The Executive Moonlighter

The Executive Moonlighter

Building Your Next Career Without Leaving Your Present Job

David R. Eyler, Ph.D.

A James Peter Book
James Peter Associates, Inc.

John Wiley & Sons

New York • Chichester • Brisbane • Toronto • Singapore

Copyright © 1989 by John Wiley & Sons, Inc.

All rights reserved. Published simultaneously in Canada.

Reproduction or translation of any part of this work
beyond that permitted by Section 107 or 108 of the
1976 United States Copyright Act without the permission
of the copyright owner is unlawful. Requests for
permission or further information should be addressed to
the Permissions Department, John Wiley & Sons, Inc.
This publication is designed to provide accurate and
authoritative information in regard to the subject
matter covered. It is sold with the understanding that
the publisher is not engaged in rendering legal, accounting,
or other professional service. If legal advice or other
expert assistance is required, the services of a competent
professional person should be sought. From a Declaration
of Principles jointly adopted by a Committee of the
American Bar Association and a Committee of Publishers.

ISBN 0-471-50070-4
ISBN 0-471-50674-5 (pbk.)

A James Peter Book

Printed in the United States of America

10 9 8 7 6 5 4 3 2 1

To Rosemary, for enduring the sacrifices associated with the making of an interesting life.

Preface

There is a way to give your business dream a wholehearted try in the real world with very little risk, if you are willing to become an executive moonlighter. This book will show you how things have changed dramatically during the last decade in ways that will let you become a serious extra-effort player in the burgeoning business services segment of our economy.

I will tell you how to do this in a thoroughly professional manner, without leaving your present position and without making an oppressive financial investment. I will show you by specific examples how an actively employed managerial or professional person can exploit an inexpensive personal computer, a home telephone, and routine overnight delivery services to work after hours in the big leagues of the business community without ever feeling like—or giving the impression of being—a kitchen table operator.

From the perspective of five years as a moonlighting executive recruiter routinely doing business with multibillion dollar firms, I will explain in detail how it can indeed be done. Using my personal experience and my observations of others, this book will describe for you why it may be very wise to begin as an executive moonlighter rather than as a high-risk traditional business startup. Whether your goal is a temporary financial shot in the arm, a longer range desire to establish a business or a yearning to learn a totally new field of endeavor, The Executive Moonlighter will help you to understand why it is neither smart nor necessary to disrupt your already comfortable lifestyle and begin your independent venture cold turkey.

Executive recruiting is just one of seven dynamic and lucrative fields described in this book that lend themselves to professional level moonlighting by a person who must also continue to respect the many demands of a fulltime position. These examples tap a broad spectrum of business activity, and you will easily be able to generalize what you learn here to an endless number of other specific applications, including one certain to embrace your own unique talents, interests, and circumstances. You will have the tools, concepts and the perspectives necessary to define your own executive moonlighting venture and operate it successfully.

You will not be asked to go out of character and become someone different than who you really are or what you want to be. A change in image is certainly reasonable, if that is something you seek; but you will be cautioned to retain your present way of life and the under rated, but critical, support systems that you dare not take for granted until you can afford to replace them in an up-and-running consistently profitable business of your own.

When you finish this book it will be with a renewed respect for how much you depend on your present position in ways that range from your sense of self-worth to the employee benefits that equate to at least another one-fourth of your present salary. This will be conveyed in such a way as to stimulate cool headed caution, but not to discourage the kind of realistic initiative that is going to lead you successfully to your goals.

The approach is totally positive, and you will be encouraged to stop daydreaming about what you might be able to do and actually implement your plan in a serious way — but prudently. I want you to learn how to enter a business during limited hours, but with real world activity and profit. This book will explain how it is eminently possible for you to identify a business service like the seven I describe, either adapt it to your current knowledge and contacts or develop new ones, and begin to function meaningfully on an after-hours basis without substantial investment or risk.

My advice throughout is to do this without leases, franchises, payrolls or any of the traditional start-up obligations that so often lead to business failure. I advocate the intelligent application of skills and equipment that you either already have or can very easily acquire. You are told how to reach out to a national market of proven customers for your services and compete as seriously as your full-time counterparts who do it from an eight-to-five setting.

The ethical aspects of moonlighting are discussed and you are told how to pursue your after-hours venture without creating a conflict of interest with your employer. More companies are recognizing moonlighting as a completely acceptable practice that actually provides a needed outlet for employees who might otherwise have to leave in order to satisfy their ambitions, but you need to know and respect the unspoken rules of the game.

The Executive Moonlighter will explain to you the fresh new concept of operating on significant commercial levels as a professional in your after hours. It will tell you how it is possible to take advantage of such things as time zone differentials to expand your before-or-after office hours operating potential. Examples are given on how you can maintain contact with your clients during important closings and at other high demand times even when you are on the opposite coast attending a conference for your employer—and do it fairly without detracting from your primary obligations.

If you now hold a professional or managerial position, but yearn to try something on your own, this book will show you how to do it in an imposing way without disrupting your life and finances. It will guide you toward achieving a position of independence that will allow you to make a sensible choice about the wisdom of going full time with your tested venture or reverting to appreciating how great it is to draw a pay check and benefits—or something in between.

The only way to really know is to give it a serious try. The extra hours will be an awfully realistic simulation of the level of effort that would surely be associated with your own full-time enterprise. The significant difference for the executive moonlighter is that you will try your wings without risking the irreparable financial and career setbacks that too often accompany the ill advised plunge into a traditional business start up.

Thoroughly examine what this book has to tell you about the potential rewards of joining the expanding ranks of the executive moonlighters who are making their mark every day in the world of commerce. Respect the insights that are revealed in the coming chapters and you will greatly reduce the risks and increase your chances of success as you proceed to actually put those great ideas of yours to the test. Inhibitions such as undercapitalization and well founded misgivings about the wisdom of risking everything can be set aside if you will proceed first as an executive moonlighter. Let me show you how it's done!

DAVID R. EYLER

Washington, D.C.
June 1989

Contents

Introduction	1
1. When Your Present Job Isn't Enough	7
2. The New Moonlighters	25
3. Considering the Possibilities	33
4. Executive Recruiter	45
5. Syndicator	77
6. Money Broker	91
7. Expert Consultant	105
8. Professional Speaker	117

9.	Seminar and Trade Show Promoter	127
10.	Computer-Related Services	135
11.	Success Stories	145
12.	Business Basics	157
13.	Ethical Considerations	167
14.	Sources of Additional Information	173
	Bibliography	185
	Index	189

Introduction

Things can be done today that were unheard of a decade ago. The way business is practiced in many professions and industries is totally different from the past. You can pick up a prestigious regional magazine and read four-color cosmetic plastic surgery advertisements by board certified physicians. Prescription eyeglasses can be provided "…in about an hour…" in major cities by retail laboratories. Legal, dental, and emergency medical services are available during extended hours in storefront settings. National telephone directories are published that list toll-free numbers for thousands of business and consumer-oriented companies that have found it advantageous to trade in a broader marketplace. Totally new ways of doing business have been developed that are very profitable and successful for the innovators who have had the courage to break the mold of tradition in their various specialties.

In the chapters that follow I will tell you how these changed conditions make it feasible for you to take your talents and ambition to the marketplace while maintaining the essential base of your present career position. The picture of the moonlighting worker as the struggling blue-collar guy who drags himself from one eight-hour shift to the next is no longer accurate. Today's moonlighter is just as likely to be a professional colleague who has found a way to extend his services to a market as yet untouched by his employer—perhaps by reaching beyond the geographic limits exploited by his company, or maybe by choosing to provide a service that isn't even close to what he does for the firm that cuts his regular paycheck.

The kinds of endeavors this book describes go well beyond the hobby or amateur levels. I am talking about setting yourself up to provide the same quality business services being performed by the traditionalists in their corporate settings, and at the same price. When I speak of executive recruiting, for example, as a moonlighting venture, it is with the full expectation that you will do what I have done and place $100,000-a-year senior officers with multibillon dollar firms for fees approaching one-third of their first-year salary. I will explain how to do this without giving up the security and stature of your present professional or management position.

The only difference you should expect to note between your endeavors and those of your full-time counterparts is the number of hours you have to devote to the quest. You will operate over the full spectrum of the working day and well beyond it, just like the competition, the main difference being that your most intense effort will be after or before the normal business hours for your full-time position. If that entails working with different time zones, so be it. Such things are not real limitations in the modern market where providers approach buyers from every corner of the nation.

Executive moonlighting can embrace a range of activities and levels of effort that are as broad or restricted as you want to make them. The motivations of its practitioners vary from wanting to experience the thrill of implementing a brilliant idea they haven't been able to sell at the office, to the very practical goal of bringing in enough extra fees to build an investment portfolio or take an extravagant vacation. You are the person to define what executive moonlighting will mean to you and just what will spell success. Failure is something that you should not experience since the resources committed are limited and controlled. The venture should be a success even if you elect to terminate or redirect it because you will have gained valuable personal insights at very little cost—and you will have the luxury of making any needed adjustments from the comfort of your ongoing career.

The changed world that makes this all possible for you is largely a technological one. For a thousand dollars or so you can acquire a respectable personal computer that will produce acceptable business correspondence, do the necessary recordkeeping, and much more. By eventually increasing that level of investment you can progress from a passable system right on up to a very sophisticated one capable of commercial-level applications for between $5,000 and $10,000.

Many managers and professionals have such equipment sitting on their desks at the office and have no problem making prudent after-hours use of it for a reasonable number of personal applications. Another approach is to buy an inexpensive compatible unit for home office use and settle for a draft printer. Final copies can be made at printing centers where laser printers are becoming as common as the copying machines they so closely resemble.

With the computer ready to support you with the kinds of correspondence and reports you and your clients are accustomed to seeing, you are ready to round out the operational picture. What used to be handled by correspondence is now taken care of by telephone in an increasing number of instances. Growing postal and office support personnel costs have combined with reduced telephone costs in the long-distance markets to justify what everyone probably preferred all along: an environment where presentations and feedback are immediate.

As an after-hours operator with little or no clerical support beyond your own two hands, the desirability of doing business by phone is even more apparent. There is also an immediacy associated with a business call that gets attention not commanded by a passive letter. The opportunity to establish the personal credibility lacking in correspondence is particularly valuable to you as a new provider reaching to the client from across the miles.

What you need in the way of telephone services is really pretty simple. You already have a telephone in your home and probably carry a telephone credit card. That alone will get you started. If the home phone needs to be extended to a study or some private area, you can do so at minimal expense.

The same is true for a second line, which may be needed to project a business image on incoming calls. That can be accomplished by having the business number answered by a distinct, businesslike message on a machine that you can page remotely from the office or on the road and returning calls as promptly as most other busy executives. The fact that you are busy with other things is none of their concern, and it will never be a factor as long as you are providing a service they value.

Without dwelling on the detailed aspects of sophisticated technology readily available at consumer prices, let me just establish for you that there is enough on the market to equip a perfectly professional after-hours business that can range the country efficiently with a solid image and service response—at very reasonable costs. In every category, from word processors to answering machines, you can start with something that is adequate but modest and progress to the sophisticated options that are there for you when they are justified by compelling business reasons and adequate cash flow.

One of the glorious things about being an executive moonlighter is that you call the shots. You are free to make the judgments—good and bad—that will ultimately make your venture succeed or fail. Erich Fromm, the eminent psychologist, once wrote a whole book on the topic entitled *Escape from Freedom*. Its premise was that man thinks he wants to have the freedom to make all of the choices in his life, but may actually be more comfortable having someone else impose most of them.

You will learn many such things about yourself as you become an executive moonlighter. It is an extremely valuable opportunity for self-exploration. I want to encourage your ambition, but also show you how to exercise it vigorously and realistically without closing options or burning bridges that may still have a legitimate place in your long-term plans. There is no more valid self-knowledge than that gained by actual experience. Executive moonlighting will provide you with the arena in which to learn real lessons with minimal risk.

Take the challenge of your business seriously and put your full energies into it, but be prepared to include among the acceptable outcomes the possibility that you personally function better in a world that does not require all the choices of running your own enterprise. For some, that will be the case; and knowing that much about yourself will be an asset that can heighten your success even if you choose to refocus on the more traditional pursuits of life. Executive moonlighters preserve such options, and I encourage you to avail yourself of that safety net.

There is a whole continuum of possibilities for balancing traditional and after-hours endeavors. For some, the moonlighting experience will light a fire that soon outshines anything they ever dreamed of accomplishing within the confines of someone else's firm. For others, it will provide just the degree of personal expression and extra income needed to make the traditional career a comfortable thing to maintain while safely experiencing a satisfying degree of personal success on the side. Still others will find private enterprise an alien world in which unacceptable pressures exist that simply could not have been appreciated until they were actually experienced. For all of these different individuals, I offer a sophisticated and yet controlled approach to exploring your second most frequently occurring real-life fantasy: What would it be like to run your *own* company?

Chapter 1

When Your Present Job Isn't Enough

What in the world has come over you anyway? You have a perfectly respectable career, a vested retirement plan, an income that is growing annually, and a lot of security besides! What is all this talk about starting a business of your own—or getting into sales or consulting or private practice or anything that will let you leave the organization behind?

The feelings that prompt such questions are not new, and they surely are not restricted to any one stage of the career life cycle. You may very well need a change in what you do for a living. That could range anywhere from a parallel move—often change for the sake of change—to something radically different from what you do now and how you presently live.

Before you do something irreversible that you might regret in a few months, consider the alternative of executive moonlighting as an ideal way to vent your frustrations in the short run—and in the long run allow you to make a well conceived change, if that proves justified. A *second* job of your own design under your own supervision may be a workable alternative to the notion of chucking it all and not looking back.

WHO YOU ARE DOES MAKE A DIFFERENCE

The dream of making a new start—escaping the sometimes stifling confines of the corporate organization—is a compelling one. But be careful. You may be underestimating how dependent your confidence, place in the community, and self-esteem are on what you get up and do each day.

Instead of taking a high-risk plunge into the all-too-often dark waters of an entrepreneurial business startup, let an executive moonlighting venture allow you to test your plan and establish a successful operating base. Don't leap over the great divide. Build a bridge, one that will allow you to safely and confidently make the move from employee to self-employed, while enjoying the best of both worlds.

You are someone not unaccustomed to a decent standard of living. Chances are you have grown used to some solid upper middle-class comforts as you progressed through your college years and the early stages of your management or professional career. You are not the sort of person who would adapt easily to living over the store or being viewed by those you encounter in your daily rounds as anything less than what you are now.

Whether or not you have given it serious thought, your work more nearly defines your station in life and how you feel about yourself than anything else you do or have. You may miss that sense of identity as much as the paycheck if you abruptly leave it behind.

When it comes right down to it, the standard of living to which you have become accustomed just isn't very negotiable. This is doubly true if there are others whose comfort and security depend on your actions. You, and those who are important in your life, are counting on not going backwards—even for a short time.

HAVING IT ALL

The challenge you face is how to go forward and realize the potential you know you have without putting everything you already enjoy at unreasonable risk. Everything has its price, but with the executive moonlighting method that price will be paid more in time and energy than in legal tender. Your pact with the devil of personal ambition will involve sacrificing time, space, and resources in order to take a shot at having a whole lot more of all these things.

My counsel is to keep your present career and make the requisite sacrifices on the side as an executive moonlighter. Let your second job displace some leisure time, money for extra things, and space for a home office, not your career—the bedrock of your lifestyle, confidence, and security.

Because you are an already successful professional person whose hands grasp the upper rungs of the ladder, it makes little sense to let go now and chance a nasty fall. With very little risk and disruption you can take a second job, one with a real difference: a quiet, low-profile application of your special talents that will be performed in such a way as not to risk your present position. As later chapters will demonstrate, it can be framed in your own or an unrelated industry, close to home or in another geographical market, during business hours where you live or in another time zone. The possibilities are infinite.

If you are that special breed of individual who needs to maintain an ambitious, traditional career and simultaneously pursue something uniquely your own, your second job should provide a taste of another way of living and working. It is an opportunity to intentionally extend yourself—your energies, talents, and resources—in order to experience *that something more* you know is out there waiting. Life *should* not and *need* not reach its conclusion with such bold dreams untested. You *can* have it all. This book will tell you how.

SECOND JOB, NOT SECOND-CLASS EFFORT

Everything is a matter of perception, and second jobs have a bad name that is undeserved. As an executive moonlighter, you will take your second job as seriously as the one you now have and hopefully will keep for a while longer, perhaps indefinitely. You will be a solo act, at least in the beginning, so the image you project can be exactly the one you want to project. You don't leave the pride, professionalism, and prestige of your corporate identity behind—you transfer it.

When I recruit top-level financial managers and place them with major investment houses, I am not some novice or ne'er-do-well laboring in a small apartment somewhere, randomly calling managers in the hope that someone will speak to me. I am a purposeful professional person playing a recognized role in a carefully selected segment of the marketplace.

For those few hours of the day, I am unquestionably qualified to operate in my clients' specialty. I am meeting an important need and competing vigorously for a substantial fee. A lesser attitude would never work.

The fact that resumes and correspondence are prepared on my own word processor instead of by a secretarial pool has no negative effect on my success. None of my clients minds that I answer my own telephone. More than a few very senior managers have spoken to my answering machine and within an hour or two had their problems solved by me from a telephone in some distant airport.

Those I serve know they have the heart, soul, and best efforts of someone totally committed to filling their requirements the way they want them filled. They read that quality in me as quickly as they would with any full-time recruiter in a high-rent office down the street or across the nation. They never know or care how intensely I work or how concentrated are my calling hours as long as their needs are met.

No one is interested in doing business with a hacker, whether he plies his trade full or part time. *Your* clients will judge *you* not by how many hours a day you sit in your office or where that office might be, but by how you do business, and how successfully you meet their needs.

Your mental attitude must be that of a deadly serious businessperson whose success truly depends on providing the best possible service or product. If you meet that challenge, it won't be long before this sideline you've begun outpaces—in income and personal fulfillment—the job you've wisely retained to sustain you until your real ambitions prove themselves.

Establishing and maintaining a professional image, even while operating from a corner in your living room, is easily and inexpensively done with modern technology. Think of how many personal and business services you buy regularly without conventional personal contact. You very likely spend thousands—perhaps millions—of your employer's dollars purchasing products or services from someone who is only familiar to you as a voice on the telephone!

Personal face-to-face contact during regular business hours by a traveling executive in a business suit is not the required norm for many of today's in-demand business services. You, too, can provide needed services efficiently through your knowledge of your market, product, or service by taking advantage of the modern ways of communicating with anyone from anywhere.

A local answering service can take your calls personally in your name. You can hire an 800-number answering service anywhere in the country—at a fraction of the cost of installing your own toll-free line—if that becomes important to the business you have chosen to pursue. In most cases a properly used answering machine will be perfectly acceptable.

You can check for messages and return your calls discreetly and professionally even while "on the job" from eight to five. Clients don't need to know—and for that matter don't care—where you're calling from. Conversely, as long as you are meeting your objectives and performing as expected in your primary job, you can rightly consider these calls just another part of the overall flow of your normal, busy work day.

The fact of the matter is that it is entirely possible to blend a number of serious efforts into the efficient flow of a single business day. Get off an airplane in any busy terminal and glance at the rows of productive people chattering away at the banks of pay phones. Who are they talking to and how long does it take? Which calls are personal and which are company business? No one knows or cares, as long as the job gets done.

Make your executive moonlighting venture a very real test of your worth in the marketplace. There is no basis for viewing yourself as some lesser functionary operating out of your own back pocket. You will be what you choose to be and grow at a rate governed by your own talents and energies. It will be unabashedly "real world," and it better not be second rate if you plan to succeed. Your image as an executive moonlighter should be a constant source of unspoken pride. If you implement it properly, you will be the only one who will know it is a second job!

TECHNOLOGY MAKES IT POSSIBLE

You are fortunate to be facing the challenges of executive moonlighting today. It has only been in recent years that the modern tools of the trade have become available at popular prices. A smart, ambitious person with a service or product to sell and a surplus of personal energy can succeed as an executive moonlighter thanks principally to two developments unique to the 1980s:

- Technical and mass marketing breakthroughs in communications and information processing that let you play in the big leagues with an unassailably professional image, from the sidelines, part time, at relatively low expense, with a low profile, from anywhere and to nearly any market!

- A services-oriented economy that welcomes your participation without questions as long as you are competent, knowledgeable in your field, respectful of common business protocols, and can deliver what is wanted, when it is wanted, at a competitive price.

In this environment, you have both the markets to serve and the means to reach them. For example, you can monitor your home-based business telephone line from anywhere in the world without needing so much as a compact beeper to page it. It is all done from a touch-tone telephone, and you will even be able to hang up without incurring long-distance charges if no messages await you. Such answering devices now cost less than $75. That same telephone line can connect your computer to vast electronic libraries of information or to a low-cost "mail box" that can accumulate messages for you to read and respond to at will.

THE HOME OFFICE

Regardless of the specialty you choose to pursue as an executive moonlighter, there is new, off-the-shelf technology becoming available daily that will make your operation more efficient and its part-time character even less apparent. Computers, modems, copiers, high-quality printers, and fax machines allow you to equip your office with total technology for only a few thousand dollars. By simply writing a check on your money market account or your home equity line of credit, you can be the one hiding behind the curtain, furiously pushing buttons and pulling levers, and giving the illusion of "the Mighty Oz."

THE MOTIVATION TO MOONLIGHT

One job may not be enough for you for a number of good reasons. It will be revealing to consider some of the classic situations that have led to moonlighting career alternatives. Any one of them, or several in combination, may fit your circumstances now or in the future. They represent a powerful array of choices that you might well adapt to personal needs. The assurance of knowing that alternatives exist is a comforting basis for your own planning. So let us consider why one job isn't enough for many different kinds of people.

The Quiet Tester

Executive moonlighting is the method of choice for many professionals who have an idea worthy of development, but one that does not yet warrant full-time exploitation. It has become a category of second job that gives its followers what they need most: a real-world testing ground for their venture that provides both full control and the anonymity necessary to continue their main career without disruption.

The quiet tester enjoys the classic privileges of the executive moonlighter. These include a very cost-effective operating environment and the prerogative of pacing the project to suit its developmental nature. Other often unrecognized benefits are an ability to stay in the mainstream of professional activity if their moonlighting venture relates to their primary industry. Even unrelated pursuits can benefit from the manager's continued exposure to the overall dynamics of the world of commerce—compared with the isolation that comes with severing the ties to take the plunge full time.

Satisfaction Missing

One of the most obvious motivations for seeking a new job, or adding a second one, is the search for the feeling of accomplishment and personal satisfaction that is not being provided by your career at its present stage of development. Executive moonlighting at a second job can provide a very rational outlet for such feelings. It can also allow you to tolerate an essentially good primary occupation until certain temporary obstacles disappear and you achieve the satisfaction you seek. It's a favorable alternative to making a hasty and unadvisable parallel move out of frustration.

For some, the second job serves as an outlet for the excess energy and talent they cannot release in their present position. Bright, capable employees are held back for many reasons. Often, the desire for more responsibility and challenge is interpreted by others as an infringement on their turf. Your coworkers and superiors may be more interested in maintaining the status quo than accommodating your ambition.

Many would-be fast trackers discover that their employer is

opposed to letting them burn along at top speed spewing forth ideas and effort faster than they can be absorbed into the established way of doing things. There is an unspoken, required pace for the expression of genius and ambition. If you are one who doesn't care to see gray in your hair before you see the initials "V.P." in your title, executive moonlighting allows you to leapfrog into the president's seat—even if it is as president of a one-person show.

Thus, by creating an outlet for your talent and energy in the realm of executive moonlighting, you fulfill your need to perform without getting into trouble within the organization. You also have the satisfaction of letting the corporate organization that stifles you finance your escape, when you're ready, into a successful enterprise.

Boredom Setting In

There is another slant on the "satisfaction needed" reason. It occurs when a company simply does not need you to contribute more. For reasons sometimes unclear, large organizations happily retain and reward people who have jobs they can perform splendidly with their eyes closed before it is time for the first coffee break. That sounds like an enviable situation, but for the bright person with ambition it's more frustrating than being overworked.

In such a situation, you find yourself daydreaming on the job. A very productive person, your worth to the company is unquestioned; but sometimes you feel a little guilty because it is all so easy. There are times on business trips when you find it totally unnecessary to burn the midnight oil in preparation for the next day's presentation.

As a matter of fact, on the plane, waiting for your baggage, standing in the rental car line, you have thoughts that go beyond the company whose corporate card you carry. Sitting in the conference room the next morning, you find it is all becoming very routine. While you don't really dislike what you are doing, you realize you're beginning to seek ways to add a new challenge to the game you play so successfully for your company.

For many bright people who populate the corporate ranks, there is usually no short-term outlet for such energies. They are counseled to be patient for the next career door to open. They are expected to continue performing well and wait their turns to reach for the next rung on the ladder.

If your internal career clock tells you the next step is an unacceptably long way away, you have the choice of making a career move that could upset your equilibrium at home and on the job. Executive moonlighting, on the other hand, lets you go on enjoying the pleasures and perks of your easy executive lifestyle while you direct your energies to breaking new ground for yourself.

No matter how subliminal, one of these three scenarios probably played a role in putting this book in your hands. The idea of expanding your career horizons beyond your present endeavors is very likely the outgrowth of some sort of self-appraisal that prompted any or all of the following revelations:

- "Wait a minute! Unless I'm a real exception to the rule, I can see the handwriting on the wall. I see how this career is likely to develop and, ultimately, end. There is a very good chance I'll end up like so 'n so, getting my gold watch as a such 'n such!"

- "There is a real inertia in organizational life—I can feel it. We all have a time, a place, and an expected role to play. I am cautioned to wait my turn, pressured to recognize my place at given points in my career and limit my behavior to that deemed suitable to the role at hand."

- "The realities of executive life aren't so terrible. Many people see them as an acceptable price to pay for the relatively good life they bring. I am different enough, however, to want to experience the freer side of life. There has to be some way to protect my traditional role and still fulfill my strong desire to attempt a walk on the entrepreneurial high wire."

Such are the musings of a budding executive moonlighter. The present career is too good to toss aside, but there is plenty of room to exercise some personal ambition in a second endeavor. For such an individual—you, perhaps?—one job is just not enough.

Storm Clouds Rising

There are still other personal reasons why a professional person might entertain the notion of executive moonlighting. One job may not be enough for a very pragmatic reason. It is not always the luxury of compensating for unfulfilled ambition that brings you to the decision.

The same high technology and rapid change that make it *possible* to start a sophisticated side business might also be making it *necessary* to do so. This is an age when many jobs become outmoded long before the jobholder's years as a breadwinner are through—before a family is raised, a mortgage retired, or a career completed (Bamford, 1986).

You don't have to be exceptionally astute to recognize the signs. If you sense that your career is in decline and you do not elect to ride it to the bottom, starting an executive moonlighting occupation now is an intelligent option. With some careful analysis of what you do well—and like to do—it may be possible to map out a successful executive moonlighting venture that can develop while the current job and benefits are still there to facilitate the transition (Kiechel, 1986).

Outplacement is a term that has become a standard part of the corporate vocabulary in the 1980s. It has spawned a thriving growth industry of companies that specialize in easing professional personnel out of their present positions with minimum loss of face and without bad feelings toward the employer saying farewell.

Although many are grateful for the chance to make a traditional change at such a time in their careers, others might better use their golden parachute time as cover for starting the business they always dreamed of—a business that now presents itself as a better way to adapt to a forced career change than starting over in a new industry in a less than desirable part of the country. Using the facilities and income provided by their employers—perhaps even limited early retirement income—newly furloughed executives find executive moonlighting can lead to the independence and dignity they seek at this stage of their lives.

Retirement Considerations

For some, the prospect of leaving daily responsibilities behind is a delight to behold. Others dread it as a boring phase of inactivity and uselessness. Still others will reach retirement age without the financial resources to sustain the lifestyle they have come to enjoy.

Under any of these circumstances, the prospect of impending retirement can be a reason to consider executive moonlighting. If it is already a reality, retirement can be the full-time job while moonlighting provides the prudent way to develop a desired business at a stage of life when risk should be minimized.

Another approach to the retirement issue is to prepare for *never* quitting, if that is your wish, even though your work in a traditional organization must end. By entering the ranks of the executive moonlighters earlier in your career, leaving the ritual eight-to-five world can be nothing more disruptive than shifting the emphasis from the long-term career to your well established sideline.

A Change in Lifestyle

Variations from the traditional employed lifestyle may be important to you. Some people grow unhappy with such things as having to live in highly resalable houses in anticipation of the next move. There are still other facts of the corporate gypsy's life that are disturbing to some.

What happens when you reach the point in life when you want to live on the beach somewhere—or near the ski slopes? If you are to remain in the corporate milieu, chances are you'll have to content yourself with periodic visits. While it is always possible to forget your corporate ties and become an innkeeper or the like, don't overlook your potential for identifying a segment of your market and using your knowledge and talents along with modern technology to serve it from a remote location (Atchison, 1986).

The best way to do just that is to test your venture on the side until it is shaken down sufficiently to make the transition a comfortable one. Learn your start-up lessons and establish a client base from the comfort of the executive moonlighting world. The price you'll pay in leisure time lost now will be more than compensated in the assurance of survival and success in your chosen setting.

A variation on this theme is the person weary of corporate relocations because he has found his spot and seeks stability, not because he longs for an idyllic life somewhere else. The opportunities exist for advancement within the corporation, but only if you move on, and on, and on. Perhaps, to your surprise, you have landed in a place you like. The family is happy there. There is a strong desire to settle down, but you realize what that means in terms of career progression: It is essentially over if you opt to remain.

A sensible solution to this dilemma is the development of a growth option that can be exploited from your present location. In such an environment, you can rationally identify and then cultivate some marketable aspect of your present skills. You may find you can provide some special service that may never have made it as a traditional small business startup on Main Street, but which succeeds beautifully in a regional or national market when you approach it without the up-front burdens and overhead of a less targeted application.

Marriage-Enhancing Considerations

There is another situation increasingly common in the 1980s that might justify a second job: the two-career couple that would like to avoid the recurring sacrifices one must make for the career of the other. Relocation is often a problem for spouses pursuing separate professional careers. A second job of the moonlighting executive variety for one or both members can be the answer ("Dual Careers," 1987).

One approach is to launch a venture in which your two sets of skills can complement each other in a single firm of your own—or two independent ones, if you prefer not to risk working together. The many possibilities here are limited only by the imaginations of the individuals involved and their ability to read the market accurately.

Another way executive moonlighting solves the two-career couple dilemma is when the more independent of the two establishes, and eventually makes the transition to full-time work in, an endeavor not limited by geography. When the spouse of an established consultant, speaker, executive recruiter, or similar professional whose client base can be served from wherever they may be faces relocation, there is minimal disruption in the second career. It might even open up new territory and opportunities, not to mention the genuine satisfaction that a certain personality type takes in achieving success on one's own terms outside of organizations.

Still another incentive for pursuing a second job on the professional level is to allay the discontent of a spouse without disrupting your livelihood and taking unreasonable risks. If your one job is creating problems in your relationship—because of too much travel, too little pay, incompatible associates, unsatisfactory social demands—executive moonlighting may be the first step toward a satisfactory solution (Machan, 1987).

Personal Fund Raising

A moonlighting venture can also be used to provide a measured, short-term financial boost for any of a number of reasons. If you take the trouble to perfect an effective moonlighting pursuit, you can have the proverbial golden egg-laying goose residing right there in your own study.

Consider the case of the person with a great investment scheme who needs ten thousand dollars to risk. Or someone who wants to take a very special vacation in style. Perhaps a new car that would be an uncomfortable extravagance unless you pay cash.

On the less frivolous side, there may be medical bills or a serious debt load from a failed business venture or bad investment. You can construct your own list of reasons to need a one-time, or periodic, financial shot in the arm that your regular employment just cannot provide. Executive moonlighting can be the answer if you have now, or are willing to learn, the necessary refinements to apply your existing talents and knowledge to the broader world around you.

Meeting Special Needs

If you are constrained by a physical characteristic that limits you in the face-to-face mode of doing business, there is an excellent chance you can overcome such limitations in several of the fields I will describe. A physical handicap resulting from a mid-career accident or illness, for example, is not going to prevent you from being the world's greatest executive recruiter, if you have the ability to think and communicate effectively by telephone.

This is but one of many such circumstances where an important career adjustment can be made successfully with the help of the executive moonlighter approach. It is highly compatible with vocational rehabilitation, if the traumatic event has caused the loss of regular employment and you are in a situation where retraining under the auspices of an established program is a possibility.

INSURING THE HAPPY ENDING

Your ultimate goal may be to establish a full-time business when the moonlighting executive phase has progressed to the point where such a move is justified. That is seldom done without needing credit and other financial relationships. Nothing will be more impressive to your banker or venture capital lender when that time comes than to show them the books on the business you started from your study a few years back that is now begging for expansion. It is no longer an untested idea, and you are not a dreamer in a business suit explaining why your lack of a track record in the enterprise should not be a barrier to lending you the money.

Instead you will be a respected client with a traditional financial record of sound credit based on years of solid employment, a history of mortgage and other payments reliably made, *and* a record of steady growth in the business you've been nurturing quietly until it emerged as something very promising. The track record is there. Satisfied clients are available as references, and you are in a position to demonstrate convincingly how adequate capitalization and full-time effort will more than replace your professional income, give employment to others, and generally benefit everyone concerned.

That is the scenario you want to construct, not the "let's do it all now with a second mortgage, the proceeds from the retirement fund, and any savings we can muster because I know it will work" group. To accomplish the former and avoid the latter, you will almost certainly decide that one job is not enough. At least not for now. Not until you start ringing those phones in the real world in your own name. It can be done in the late twentieth century with little more than a good idea, a lot of guts, and a will to be your own person.

There are many things you will never anticipate adequately, and there is so much to be learned in starting a business, that you owe it to yourself to maintain the sort of safety net that will let you face the dilemmas with sufficient staying power—psychic and financial—to weather the storms. As an executive moonlighter you will keep your identity as a professional person with a solid place in the world of work—and still have the privilege of going forward with your own pursuits.

You will retain the infrastructure that is so vital to your day-to-day existence as a responsible citizen—various kinds of insurance, sick days with pay, paid vacation, the basis for your credit, linkages to others in your field, unspoken status considerations that are reinforced every day as you make your commute, enter your building, and function in a group in which you have an acceptable identity. These are the subtle things that keep a spring in your step and the essential level of confidence in your heart. You want to preserve them until they are replaced by success in your own right.

Some of these potential losses can be overcome with adequate financing. Others have no dollar value. Unless you have personally experienced it, there is no way that anyone else can tell a well paid professional person with an ample niche in life's pecking order and who is accustomed to a very comfortable lifestyle—someone with a schedule, places to be, people who ask for your advice, assurances that your bills will be paid and further credit extended when you need it—what it feels like not to have all of that. You can buy insurance and some of the other things, but no price can be attached to the self-image, fundamental security, and sense of self-worth that are so much an outgrowth of your current employment. Executive moonlighting covers these vital bases for you as you make the transition.

The chances are good that comfortable success won't come overnight. You will probably blunder, do some dumb things, experience some large ego blows, and generally need some reinforcement that isn't found in a one-person office.

For these reasons and more, one job is not enough for you right now. You need two. One to continue to provide what you probably don't yet realize how very much you'll miss, and another to start you down that road of self-expression that will eventually find you the captain of your own successful enterprise.

Chapter 2

The New Moonlighters

The old moonlighter was someone with a second job who was trying to make ends meet. The new moonlighter is a professional person with a fire in his or her gut that isn't being allowed to burn freely in the confines of an institutional career. Extra effort and energy are required of both, but most of the similarities end there. The new executive moonlighters are aiming high and applying both the energy and specialized knowledge that promise to make life richer for them and those they may eventually employ.

Generally, they have logged at least several years on the floor of some established organization. In that environment, they usually were fast studies who broke the code quickly and were ready to surge ahead. At that point, they encountered limitations of institutional life that frustrated them to the point of looking for another path in which to channel their talents and energies.

The difference between the executive moonlighter and the classic breakaway entrepreneur of old is that today's bright minds are found in bodies accustomed to a level of good living they are reluctant to leave behind as they establish themselves as independent achievers. They have the good judgment to demonstrate a capacity to support independently the lifestyles to which they have become accustomed before burning their bridges behind them.

This is the person willing to give up some evenings at happy hours and health spas, but not the source of income that makes these luxuries possible. His or her approach to solving the problem of institutional frustration is not bolting to a similar position in a competing organization, but taking on an extra load, after hours, above and beyond the existing demands of a full-time professional position.

I am talking about the man or woman who already does something quite well but whose energy and imagination are not being fully exploited on the job. Such people still see plenty of opportunity to put their dreams on the market, by themselves if necessary, after hours, if need be; but they feel compelled to get them out there and operating. They are not content to languish within the organization, waiting their turn and putting their ambitions on hold.

The new moonlighters are confident they have a contribution to make and have reached the conclusion that it is going to be best made, at least in part, outside the organization. Yet they have the good sense to recognize that their place in the organization is a valuable base for networking, launching, testing, and establishing their own enterprises.

PROFESSIONALS WITH MORE THAN ONE INTEREST

According to the Bureau of Labor Statistics (BLS), as reported in the *Wall Street Journal* (Trost, 1986), nearly three out of four professionals and managers are satisfied with the status quo. The same hours and the same money are fine with them. Statistics in this article revealed that another 18 percent of those managers and professionals were willing to work longer in order to make more of themselves. That is the segment of the population from which the executive moonlighters emerge.

The same BLS survey revealed an increase in flexible working schedules, which resulted in more people spending at least eight hours a week working at home—many of them in a consulting capacity. These are the kinds of data that tend to support the assumption that ambitious professionals are finding ways to vent their energies independently without abruptly leaving their full-time positions. These are the executive moonlighters who are so difficult to identify in the traditional labor force statistics.

In the recession year of 1983, the *Wall Street Journal* (Hymowitz, 1983) gave front-page attention to moonlighting in the executive ranks. According to that article, the economic squeeze that had cut deeply into the ranks of management and professional services in industry had left in its wake a fend-for-yourself attitude that produced a lot of moonlighting. A sense of lifetime job security and blind loyalty to the organizations that employed them became a thing of the past for newly realistic executives who began to create alternatives for themselves while remaining on the corporate payrolls.

The article noted BLS surveys showing upward trends in the percentage of both professional and technical workers who reported pursuing after-hours employment. It was stressed that the figures reported (5 to 8 percent of the work force) were thought to underestimate heavily the true numbers of moonlighters. Many professional workers are not about to report to the government or anyone else that they are moonlighting. A later article (Jamal, 1988) reported that the actual statistics would probably be nearly three times the official estimates.

In their interviews with moonlighting professionals, *Wall Street Journal* reporters (Hymowitz, 1983; Trost, 1986) noted the importance of familiarity with modern technology in enabling executives to run big league sidelines effectively. The personal computer was cited most often as the tool that makes it all possible. Their reasons for burning the midnight oil professionally ran the gamut from supporting a more expensive lifestyle to increased security and personal satisfaction.

The executive moonlighter can be of any age, but it is an increasingly common phenomenon among mid-career professionals and managers who face the realities of stagnation and involuntary change. One California attorney began investing on a moonlighting basis in a chain of hair-cutting franchises, had the misfortune of seeing the franchisor go bankrupt, lost his investment, and returned to the practice of law. In reporting his story, *Forbes* (Bamford, 1986) noted that he never lost his love for moonlighting. As a sideline, he now represents franchisees in a variety of fields. Time and again it is evident that even the failed ventures of executive moonlighters provide impetus for their future successes.

The attorney's story is not unusual. Executive moonlighters tend to learn many lessons in the process of testing their entrepreneurial sea legs. It is the safest way to find a workable independent application of your talents or a permanent part-time occupation that complements your full-time profession.

Jamal's 1988 *Personnel Journal* article on moonlighters concluded there was a real need to reexamine management attitudes toward these workers. He cited studies confirming no differences between moonlighters and single-job workers in many traditional measures of employee health, happiness, stability, turnover, and job performance. In fact, the moonlighters were found to be superior employees in a number of important respects, such as high self-esteem and low anxiety.

He also noted in his research that the total work week of the modern moonlighter is less than the standard work week of a generation ago. Researchers point out that companies do not hesitate to push their managers well beyond the usual 40 hours when it serves their purpose, nor do they express concern regarding the negative effects of these extended hours. Such realities tend to dilute traditional arguments against the moonlighter.

Writers like Jamal stress that the new executive moonlighters are little different in their hours and pursuits than others who are *encouraged* by their employers to accept outside directorships, consulting arrangements, teaching posts, and activities such as contract research. These outside roles are generally considered to reflect positively on company prestige and rarely attract official criticism. The substantive differences between these activities and those pursued independently by moonlighting executives are very small and should pose little concern for conflicts of interest and lessened productivity.

Industry Week took a look at the emerging practice of executive moonlighting at the management level (Mullally, 1976). The article's findings laid an excellent base upon which to compare the state of higher-level moonlighters more than a decade later. It concluded that managers were far less apt to have second jobs than to moonlight independently. The more common practice, then and now, finds professionals pursuing some entrepreneurial application of their skills in the marketplace. In Mullally's broad definition of moonlighting, that included anyone doing anything that involved trading time and talent for money—a perfectly applicable perception in the late 1980s.

The *Industry Week* article saw the moonlighter motivated heavily by dissatisfaction and underutilization. Often, these factors were more personal in origin, rather than the fault of the employer. Today, it is recognized that human nature is so complex that moonlighting can actually be therapeutic and a boon to an executive's productivity both on and off the primary job.

The new moonlighters are your ambitious professional colleagues who may or may not reveal the fact they have another business identity outside the office. They are the people who value the lifestyles they have achieved and respect the standard organizational positions that support these lifestyles. There is a deep-seated desire to do more, however, and they have discovered that the world is their oyster when it comes to crafting a full-blown application of their business ideas in the marketplace.

From the outset of their ventures, today's moonlighters possess sufficient business acumen to intelligently plan and operate a sophisticated service business with the necessary low profile to avoid conflict of interest with, or lessened productivity on, their primary jobs. They are conversant with personal computer and communications technology and use these skills to create an impact upon the business community far beyond their local markets. Dynamic risk takers with the smarts to keep their lives in balance until they can reliably choose life in the organization, the independent life, or a self-designated balance between the two—these are the new moonlighters.

The May 1985 BLS poll of basic labor force data (*Current Population Survey*, 1985) found that, of the 106,878,000 job holders, 5.7 million were moonlighting. That amounts to 5.4 percent of all employed workers. Among them, the greatest single reason for working that second job was economic—*to earn more money*. A further examination of the data, however, shows that moonlighting for the necessities of life is less likely to occur as you progress from hourly wage workers to the professional and managerial workers who accounted for one in four of those surveyed. The executive moonlighters who are the subject of this book have more than extra income in mind as they look beyond their full-time positions.

HIGHER ORDER MOTIVATIONS

Humans are very complex creatures. Work is one of our most powerful means of expressing talent and achieving satisfaction in life. For many, that inner complexity makes it impossible to embrace a single career without feeling an urge to try something more. So, while you ponder your discontent in the work place and your motivations for trying other things, consider the possibility that you may be a person who needs more than one job for adequately expressing your personality and talents. The financial motivation associated with old-fashioned moonlighters probably doesn't begin to explain the actual forces driving the new executive moonlighter.

It has long been recognized that the higher up the economic ladder you climb, the less likely it will be that money is your primary motivator. In his 1962 book, *Toward a Psychology of Being*, Dr. A.H. Maslow had a wonderfully simple illustration for why people do the things they do. Maslow depicted the motivators of life as different levels of a pyramid, with the broad base being the bedrock necessities like food and shelter. Those who progress up this "hierarchy of needs" encounter the less essential, but eminently desirable, luxuries such as personal satisfaction and artistic achievement.

Since this book deals with *executive* moonlighting, it is, by definition, concentrating on those who have already acquired the basic necessities and are in search of the higher order satisfactions described by the late Dr. Maslow. This is a valuable perspective for those of you considering a new business venture.

I urge you to maintain a healthy respect for the value of what you have already achieved. It saddens me to see accomplished managers and professional people discard their well ordered lives for an ill considered fling at entrepreneurship. Although earning the money to acquire basic necessities may not be your motivator now, the loss of substantial capital in a failed venture can put you in a position where it will be.

Bad business judgment can pull you back down the pyramid to the level where you will be struggling for food, shelter, and financial survival—an alien and personally destructive situation for those who long ago passed that point. Executive moonlighting helps you avoid such risk.

A CASE HISTORY

Until he died at the age of 75, Wallace Stevens was an executive moonlighter toiling at the pinnacle of Dr. Maslow's hierarchy: artistic achievement. According to an article in *Pace* (Blackburn, 1988), Stevens was a man whose moonlighting was a labor of love—love of his primary employment as a vice-president in charge of actuarial statistics for a major insurance company, and love of writing poetry. For the latter, he quietly earned a National Book Award and a Pulitzer Prize, to the amazement of his coworkers. Each pursuit was a necessary part of Stevens' life. Each provided rewards that allowed him to tolerate and excel in the other, according to Dr. Rodney L. Lowman, the Duke University psychologist quoted in the article.

Your reasons for executive moonlighting may be far less esoteric than Wallace Stevens' were, but his story may very well uncover in you a similar yearning for an outlet—at least initially—that gives you personal satisfaction by supplementing your regular work rather than replacing it. This is a luxury you can preserve by joining the ranks of the new executive moonlighter.

Chapter 3

Considering the Possibilities

Executive moonlighting requires a bit of self-examination and reflection if you are going to be successful. Personal motivation is important in any kind of work and absolutely essential in an after-hours venture. The rational selection of a specialty that has a chance of succeeding is another must. A realistic appraisal of what you have to give and are willing to invest in terms of time and money are critical considerations. Finally, it will be necessary to understand what you hope to achieve. In other words, just what do you expect from your moonlighting?

YOUR INTERESTS

Make your executive moonlighting endeavor something you very much like to do. You will be devoting many hours to it, extra-effort hours spent after you have already worked a full day or on weekends when other pleasant diversions abound.

With a properly selected specialty, your moonlighting hours can be a refreshing and uplifting part of your life. The stimulation should be similar to the high experienced when you are dragging through a routine day and suddenly find yourself faced with a fresh and totally unexpected challenge. I'm talking about the sort of boost that comes with a last-minute invitation to participate in a top-level meeting or an unexpected assignment to represent the firm at a conference in Honolulu the next day—when you are sitting in the middle of a snowstorm in Chicago. One minute you couldn't be persuaded to cross town for any reason; the next you've figured out how to reach the airport in record time.

Executive moonlighting should provide the kind of welcome challenge that perks you up. The secret lies in the proper selection of activity, and *that* is a variable only *you* can control.

An evening of solitude doing research deep in an electronic database may represent the ultimate release for one person and grinding misery for another. Spending hours on the telephone making critical arrangements for a seminar may be just the thing for the right person, but a gut-wrenching chore for someone else. Executive moonlighting can embrace the full spectrum of individual business activity, and you must choose what will work for you.

If you are unsure as to where your interests lie—or have several possible interests and need help deciding which you will perform best in—call a local college counseling center or private career counselor and arrange to take an interest inventory test. Dr. John Holland's "Self Directed Search (SDS)," for example, is a self-administered set of questions designed to reveal response patterns that point you toward and away from basic kinds of activities (Holland, 1985). It will help you determine whether the things you say you like or dislike parallel those of people who are happy doing certain types of work.

Holland's test results fall into the categories "Realistic," "Investigative," "Artistic," "Social," "Enterprising," and "Conventional." In various combinations, these categories are linked to a multitude of occupations. For some, the insights gained from such a relatively simple exercise are well worth the effort. Others already know what they want to pursue. Only you can judge how to proceed. Avail yourself of this kind of guidance if you find yourself drawn to executive moonlighting but are unclear as to exactly what occupation will prove satisfying and successful for you.

SELECTING A SPECIALTY

Do not overlook the obvious in selecting the area in which you will concentrate. Your present field may be an excellent choice. The advantages can include a thorough knowledge of the industry and its business practices. Also, you're probably familiar with the directories and publications that serve as the basis for your contacts.

If you would find it awkward to moonlight in some aspect of your full-time occupation, consider reaching beyond your immediate geographical bounds and plying your trade in another region of the country. Remember, you can probably do business anywhere there is long distance telephone service. It is also possible to select a narrow specialty within your overall industry that would complement rather than conflict with your present full-time work.

You may find it either necessary or desirable to enter an entirely new field of specialization. If so, make it something that interests you and something you can do well—something you might choose if you had your career to start over again.

In providing any service to an industry, you do not have to be an expert in all facets of it. You do, however, need to have a broad sense of how the business operates, its needs, and the jargon with which its members communicate.

Whether you elect to stay with your present field or venture into a new one that you must investigate thoroughly, following are some tests that your selection should meet:

- Do potential clients within this industry currently purchase the types of services you plan to provide? To determine this, you ask: Call, send letters, conduct a survey.

- Are there sufficient trade directories and publications to help you develop a customer list? You will find it much easier to develop business in an area already sufficiently defined by directories and trade publications.

- In major metropolitan areas, the *Yellow Pages*, or the *Business-to-Business Yellow Pages*, if available, can serve this purpose well for some specialties; but a directory for the specific trade or profession is invaluable. This is such an important factor that you might even approach your selection by first determining what industries already offer strong support in the way of directories and trade organizations, and choose one of these. Whether your business plan ultimately calls for direct mail or targeted telephone contact, you will almost certainly do better if you can identify and reach your customers readily.

- Do you now have, or can you develop, a good grasp of the terminology used within this specialty? You will need to become comfortable with accepted business practices for your chosen field. What terms are used? What performance criteria are mentioned and what do they mean? What professional certifications (CPA, PE, CPC, etc.) are highly regarded? You can develop this knowledge base for almost any specialty you select. Your decision is whether to do this or operate from your current knowledge base.

- Is this an occupation and industry that hold your interest? The choice is yours, so you might as well select something that will capture your imagination and make your work enjoyable. If you always thought you might have made a good (name the profession), perhaps that's an excellent choice for you as an executive moonlighter.

If you have an occupation in mind, and it doesn't meet the tests described above, visit your local public library and research other industries and the services they purchase. The U.S. Government's *Occupational Outlook Handbook* is an annual publication that will give you an overview of a number of careers and their prospects in the labor market. Sources of further information, such as trade and professional associations, are listed at the back of each section. Write or call those you are interested in to see if you can obtain a copy of their membership directories. If they are made available to members only, can you join—perhaps as an associate member? Where could you review a current copy in your part of the country?

Some organizations are protective of their membership lists and directories. Others openly market them to raise funds and lower member dues. Using this approach, you can find a field that both interests you and promises to be a rich vein of potential business you can mine efficiently.

Throughout your investigation, I suggest that, if asked, you identify yourself as a consultant in the field, rather than someone seeking general information. You are indeed acting in a consulting capacity and there is no need to define it further. The exact nature of your project and the names of those retaining you must remain confidential at this point.

Other sources not to overlook are friends and other contacts in professions you think might interest you. Ask them if they are members of professional and trade associations. If so, see if they would allow you to review their membership directories. If such contacts are good friends, ask them to get a copy of the directory for you or loan you their previous year's edition so you can test the field for your purposes.

You can accomplish the same thing by visiting the offices of practicing members of the profession, if you handle yourself in a careful and businesslike manner. Call ahead to explain you are a consultant doing business within their profession and would appreciate being able to review their membership directory briefly before investing a hundred dollars or so in something that might not be appropriate for your purposes. Assure them you won't take any of their time if they will just leave a copy at the reception desk for you to review in their office. While you have it, determine how useful it is and jot down the address and telephone number where a copy can be obtained.

Your local public library probably also has a copy of the *Directory of Directories* (Marlow, 1987), which is an excellent source of ideas and contacts. Use it to define likely specialties and track them down in the library, at a local professional office, or by telephone.

You can also write or telephone the publishers of trade journals and ask if they publish what is known as a "directory issue." If so, ask when it was or will be published, and whether you can order a copy. One example is *Trust and Estates*, a publication for the trust banking industry. Its December edition is a detailed guide to trust departments nationwide and their principal officers. The same publisher produces a variety of useful materials in industries as varied as real estate, shopping center management, paint, fencing, and many others. Chapter 14, "Sources of Additional Information," tells you how to contact this and other such publishers.

IT PAYS TO SPECIALIZE

It is possible to be a generalist and go after business anywhere you find it, but that is not a very effective approach for the executive moonlighter. Specialization allows you to target your time and energy, and make the most efficient use possible of the hours you have available for your moonlighting venture.

Regardless of the type of business service you provide, you will probably be doing much of your work on speculation or on a contingency fee basis. There will be times when you invest many hours only to have a competitor walk away with the job, and the fee. If you are working within a narrow specialty, your efforts are not in vain. You may be able to use what you learned and contacts you made in subsequent projects.

As an executive recruiter, for example, you may uncover a candidate who doesn't fill the job at hand, but who proves perfect for a future opening. That is one big advantage of specialization, and it is of even greater importance for the part-time practitioner who probably will not turn business over quickly enough to operate efficiently in multiple specialties.

You will become an expert in your specialty, or at least in

certain aspects of it. In time, you will come to know a great deal about who occupies key positions throughout an industry. More importantly, you will come to know many of them well—if not as friends, as respected, periodic, professional contacts.

In my specialty of executive recruiting, you know either directly or by inference what many of your associates' career aspirations are. You learn their levels of experience and degree of specialization, their salary and incentive packages, and whether they are stalled in their career climb or moving up on schedule. In addition, you know compensation averages for the industry and are aware of industry events such as mergers and acquisitions. This is knowledge you accumulate in the general course of communicating with your contacts, and it is apt to be more powerful and useful if you specialize.

ACTIVELY TESTING YOUR HUNCH

You have done your research, and you know where to go with your calling card. Now it is time to explore the interiors of the industry you've selected.

You can either begin outright by marketing your particular service, or first create for yourself a brief, structured interview that will help you learn more about the inner workings of the profession. Contact people like those you believe will prove to be your clients. Again, introduce yourself as a consultant working in their field of specialization who would value their expert advice and assistance.

Ask if your proposed services are in demand. As an executive recruiter for example, you would seek the answers to the following questions:

- (To a potential recruit): Do recruiters call you to describe job openings, or is the job market in your specialty pretty tight right now?
- (To a hiring official): Do you satisfy most of your personnel needs through classified advertising, or is it common to pay

a fee to recruiters? If I had a candidate with an XYZ degree and four years of successful experience in your industry, would you be interested in learning more? If not, what minimum criteria must candidates meet?

If one lead proves to be a dead end, ask that individual who in his or her company might have a need for your services. Get a name and phone number, or two. The key to successful networking is to go away from each interview with at least two more leads. Using this method, you may discover a whole new market niche you weren't even aware of when you began sleuthing.

The overall rules of thumb governing demand for services are divided along these lines: *technical specialties* versus *performance-oriented specialties*. Technical specialties are those with a limited number of available people simply because each company has unique needs it trains people to meet; and performance specialties are those in which job holders or service providers clearly earn their keep by being great sales producers, loan generators, stock pickers, and the like. Almost every field of endeavor has these classes of people; and they are the people you must identify to create a demand for your services.

People who function in routine administrative roles, regardless of title or salary level, are just not that hard to come by; so recruiters are seldom paid to find them. The same truth applies in fields other than recruiting. Whether your specialty is consulting, brokering loans, or doing specialized research, you will succeed by serving the technical and performance-oriented areas of the companies you approach.

Do not be intimidated by the reality that others are already operating in your chosen field. You should be more concerned if they weren't! Accept the fact that anything worth doing is being done by more than one person. In general, there is always room for one more person who is *willing* to pursue the business aggressively and *able* to perform competently.

You will market your services to companies with such a pressing need that, to fill their requirements, they are willing to deal with anyone who demonstrates knowledge and professionalism. Such companies have already exhausted the easy and inexpensive methods. In the field of executive recruiting, the human resources department has run its ads and tried its favorite recruiting firms—all to no avail. There is room for you, if you can deliver. That is exactly the situation you're looking for. Search until you find it—you will.

If you encounter a company that has an exclusive purchase agreement with another firm, don't waste your time or theirs. Let them know you are available, if the situation changes; then move on to another, more open, prospect.

Don't write a company off for all time because of limitations they describe today. Their receptiveness toward you is directly proportional to their needs at the moment.

With all prospective clients, stress your contingency fee structure that costs them nothing unless you deliver. Always, display an unimpeachably professional demeanor, avoid unnecessary calls and inappropriate referrals, and you will discover plenty of opportunity out there.

YOUR COMMITMENT

None of the executive moonlighting ventures described in this book requires major financial resources. Neither do they take away your current paycheck. However, it is not possible to pursue any of them unless you can afford the additional telephone expense and a personal computer to support your efforts.

A careful assessment of what is already available at the office might make a computer purchase unnecessary, at first. If you can use the equipment at work without violating company policies, you may be able to test your moonlighting activity long enough to be certain it will justify the investment.

Unless your selected endeavor involves computer research or anything else that requires extensive access, you probably can meet your early needs by preparing a few documents on company equipment before or after your regular hours. I caution you to investigate company policy thoroughly before you choose this approach, however. Don't do anything that will jeopardize your position, draw undue attention to your sideline, or consume an excessive amount of company resources. At the same time, I encourage you to begin as simply as possible, buying equipment only after you have justified it with an initial track record of success.

Time is the resource you will use the most as an executive moonlighter. Prepare yourself, and any family members, for the loss of free time. This will become a negative only if you find yourself performing an objectionable task or if you have burdened your venture with financial pressures that make you its slave. Remember, you chose to begin as a moonlighter to avoid both these problems.

The best laid plans must still give way to the demands of your regular work and personal life. There really is a limited number of hours in the day. Be realistic about how far you can push yourself. It is far better to make your after-hours business something that can be sustained with a realistic amount of time and effort, rather than doom it with expectations you simply cannot meet.

REACHING YOUR GOAL

I thoroughly enjoy a certain television commercial that begins with a distant aerial view of a beautiful home perched on a tiny tropical island. Then the camera moves in on the lush greenery, the crashing surf below, and a happy, confident man talking on the telephone—his tall, cool drink and his personal computer sharing table space just a few feet from his swimming pool. He comes into full view just as he exclaims into the phone, "Great! We have a deal!" and hangs up with a smile. Who wouldn't smile?

Is business *really* being done this way? You bet it is! The term "telecommuting" was coined to label those fortunate people who are so in demand they can make their contributions to the world of commerce from a site of their choosing. A field that was once occupied solely by writers and wizards in esoteric specialties has broadened considerably. *Business Week* recently noted that many top executives now work where they play (Atchison, 1986). In the television commercial just mentioned, the setting was tropical. The magazine article favored a remote ski resort in Colorado. Your goal may simply be to live out a business fantasy in the evenings from the comfort of your own den.

Whatever your goal, executive moonlighting is uniquely suited to helping you achieve it. It will allow you the luxury of being almost anything you choose to be, in microcosm. Pick your hours, specialty, and market; and go for it all from the comfort of your existing support system and lifestyle. Understand there is a learning curve in all things; and apply yourself diligently, intelligently, and consistently to a thoroughly professional effort.

Luckily, you have a unique capacity for doing just that. You have the means, the education, the business experience, and the motivation to carve a niche for yourself in the world of commerce. And you can do it in a controlled, low-cost, but fully real-world way.

Your personal circumstances and degree of commitment are your only limitations. Most likely you have experience identifying and using expert opinion and research in your present full-time position. Apply those same skills to your moonlighting venture.

THE "FAST START"

A faster alternative is the immersion method. One way to do this is to identify a highly regarded training workshop or seminar in your new field and attend it on your own time and at your own expense. National associations in various fields can guide you to such an educational experience. You will return home motivated and already in touch with a network of people who will help you solve future problems. Another fast start-technique is to contract for a day or more of one-on-one training and consultation with a person already highly regarded in the field.

Regardless of the approach you take, executive moonlighting can help you reach the goals you set within the risk, dislocation, and cost parameters you find comfortable.

Chapter 4

Executive Recruiter

Read the classified section of the Wall Street Journal if you would like to get a feel for the market potentially available to people in the job placement industry. It would be misleading to imply that all these listings represent promising leads for executive recruiters. Nothing could be further from the truth. Most of the jobs are relatively easy to fill: the personnel department places an ad, applicants present themselves, the most promising are interviewed, and the best are hired. That is true for lowly jobs and lofty positions alike—more often the former, less likely the latter.

Where the executive recruiter comes in is for that roughly 20 percent of the job market not adequately served by an ad in the paper. The reasons vary. More demand than supply in a given specialty is the big one. Another is that the employer wants to hire on a less public basis—search for the best talent quietly without dealing with the crush of unscreened applicants from advertising. Some searches are too specialized to pursue via advertising. Some do not allow employers to ethically approach the people they would really love to interview. A skilled recruiter who has established relationships in an industry knows who might *like* to talk with whom and, when the opportunity presents itself, facilitates their getting together privately.

FINDING A NICHE

There are very large and dynamic search firms that serve many of the recruiting needs, especially at the higher salary levels.

That is not to say you cannot operate in the same arenas. It is really up to you. You may come into the executive search business with high-level contacts that can put you into the swing of things at the very top. If not, you will either earn your stripes and eventually develop such contacts and the confidence that goes with it, or you will choose to operate at other levels.

The major companies are generally known as *retained search* firms: They demand and receive money up front for their efforts. Sometimes it is paid in a lump sum, often it is an incremental series of payments made as the search progresses. They also receive expenses for their travel, telephone calls, business entertainment, and so on.

Some smaller firms do business this way too, but for the most part you will be more successful entering the market as a *contingency search* firm. As such, you will uncover the needs of employers, convince them that you are proficient at your craft, command their respect by being literate in the basic terminology of their industry and the position they seek to fill, then proceed with the understanding that they will accept your referrals and pay you a substantial fee if one of your people is actually employed. If they are not, the employer owes you absolutely nothing for your efforts. You work on speculation.

Contingency search is raw capitalism. You either believe in your ability to produce, or you don't. You must be successful often enough to have it all average out to a profit that satisfies you as a businessperson. It is this free-wheeling quality that makes it possible for you to enter the executive recruiting business with little more than an ability to communicate and learn.

Some companies will not deal with recruiters at all—very few, actually. Some will deal only with the premier retained

As a moonlighting executive recruiter you will:
- Select an area of specialization.
- Determine that hiring demand exceeds readily available, appropriately experienced people in that specialty.
- Determine that fees are paid by employers in that field.
- Locate directories that will enable you to identify hundreds of employers and thousands of potential recruits in your specialty.
- Identify either a viable position to fill or candidate to place and proceed to recruit to fill the position or market to place the candidate. At any given time, you will be active in either the marketing or recruiting side of this two-part cycle.
- At the point of accepting a job order, establish agreement with the employer to pay your fee and confirm it with your fee letter.
- Continue contacting employers or potential candidates until you have either filled the position or placed your candidate—OR until you have encountered a new situation that represents a more immediate chance of a successful placement and switch your emphasis to the more promising pursuit.
- Assist in arranging the interviews that you stimulate.
- Assist in resolving any differences and misunderstandings.
- Assist in making the offer and concluding the hiring.
- Bill the employer for the appropriate fee.
- Resume calling on the basis of your most promising candidate or job order, repeating the cycle endlessly.

Figure 1: An Overview of Executive Recruiting

search firms—again, few, particularly when you are talking about mid-level management and technical positions. Many of the large recruiting firms will deal only with searches involving annual salaries of $75,000 and up. It all creates a very nice opportunity for you. Understand that it is not a painless, order-taking/order-filling sort of opportunity. The rewards are just too high and the competition too intense for it to be that simple, but the opportunity is very real by any objective measure.

There are thousands of positions in the $30,000-to-$75,000 annual salary range that will be filled every month. Many will be filled by small firms and individual operators—some of them executive moonlighters—who will work very hard and collect roughly 30 percent of the candidate's annual salary as a contingency fee. That is $9000 at the low end, $22,500 at the top! The earning potential is genuinely impressive, but it is not an easy task. A lot of skill and persistence are required; but it is a viable business, and it is within your reach. You can play the game very well, and play it cost effectively from a quiet corner of your study until you can afford or desire fancier surroundings.

If it's so darned easy, why isn't everyone doing it? Try it and you will see. It is at once a very simple and a very demanding business. It is a "head" business: It puts great strain on your ego and attitude unless you are a very unusual person. This is something you can certainly learn to handle. You may be someone who is not really affected negatively by the ambiguous nature of the recruiting business, but for most people it does create a strain.

You will ever need to worry about everyone jumping into your business *and staying there* as your long-term competition. Studies commissioned by major firms in the industry try to explain why people earning excellent livings and working in very nice offices quit for lesser jobs. The answer is the psychological stress of constantly trying to structure a high-return deal that is totally dependent on not one or two, but at least three sets of human behavior—the employer's, the candidate's, and your own. While there are many variables you cannot control, you often feel you must try and generally fault yourself when a five-figure fee disintegrates before your eyes.

For many, the opportunities and freedom associated with independent executive recruiting far outweigh these perils; but I do want to make you aware of them as you consider this approach to being an executive moonlighter. If you *can* perform in this environment, no opportunity I know of offers a greater return in fewer actual working hours and with a lower business investment.

HOW TO BEGIN

As you establish your executive recruiting practice, you will face a one-time problem that literally will never occur again. There is a "... which comes first, the chicken or the egg?" problem that you encounter momentarily during the start up. You must have either a job order for which to recruit or a candidate to market, in order to be in business. The problem is a fleeting one, so I will suggest several approaches to solving it:

1. You may be operating in your own field. If that is so, you probably know of someone who would like to explore the job market. Use that person's background to begin a marketing cycle.
2. You may be willing to consider an ideal position yourself and have qualifications in the field of choice. If so, market yourself initially.
3. You know of a job that needs to be filled in your speciality. You get a job order and proceed to recruit for it.

As your business progresses, you will be talking with more people in the field—making your marketing and recruiting calls. Some will have little time for you, others will respond to your inquiries more fully. By taking the trouble to ask the right questions beyond your immediate objective, you will regularly discover that they plan to hire in the future, or they would hire a certain kind of person if they could find him or her, but they are not ready to launch an active search. Perhaps the person you talk with volunteers that she or he is open to another opportunity, will provide a résumé, and welcomes your efforts on his or her behalf as you go about your business.

This cycle of activity will leave you with no shortage of situations you can exploit until better opportunities come your way. Perhaps they are less than ideal, not high-priority items, but they are good enough to keep you calling until the better opportunity reveals itself.

In all cases, you are not in the business of disclosing candidates' names and positions until you have confirmed with them that they have an interest, so what you are marketing are sets of qualifications and experience. Only when the person on the other end shows genuine interest do you give further details, and you never disclose identity or place of present employment until you've cleared it. You could get someone fired and face a lawsuit. You must never resort to inventing jobs or candidates. That is known as ruse calling, and it can be illegal.

Stay honest. There is simply no good reason to misrepresent yourself. There are endless jobs to be filled and people who would consider a change. Your task is to sort out the priority ones and devote your limited time to the candidates who have convinced you that they would *really* accept a new position and the hiring officials who have a *genuine need* that they *will act* upon when you produce the right person. At the beginning and during lean times, devote genuine effort and interest to your weaker leads, but always be prepared for the associated activity to lead to more urgent business.

MARKETING THE CANDIDATE

Marketing is the process of presenting a candidate to potential employers, briefly and in confidence, in hopes they will either consider that person for employment or reveal other needs to you. If they express another urgent need, you will be faced with the decision of continuing what you are doing or switching gears—it's the kind of problem you like to have. As your knowledge of people in the field grows, you may have another alternative; going to your memory or files and coming up with a person or two who does not fit your current need but is just right for the new requirement, or who might be worth calling to see if they know of other potential candidates.

This gives you some idea of (1) how the business cycle feeds on itself, and (2) the tremendous importance of staying active in your calling. One thing leads to another, even when you don't expect it or it seems to be unrelated. In terms of the actual process, here is exactly what you do:

- Learn the necessary facts about a worthy candidate during a structured telephone interview with that individual.

- Prepare a marketing script that introduces you and your purpose to the potential employer briefly (less than one minute), but thoroughly, stressing the candidate's characteristics most likely to elicit interest from the person called.

- Have your candidate's detailed information at hand in case you are asked for more than you have presented.

- Prepare a list of likely prospects to call who might reasonably have an interest in hiring the kind of person you intend to present. If you have a good directory or have been working long enough to know your contacts, that list will contain names and direct numbers. If not, it will contain company names and main switchboard numbers. You will have to work your way to the appropriate person and make note of who it is to expedite future searches.

In most cases, you are better advised to call the hiring official than the personnel office, unless you have an established relationship with someone there. You may end up working with personnel, and they can be great people to do business with once they know you and have reason to work with you, but they often will not respond to a random marketing call unless they have an urgent need. The hiring official (the prospective employee's potential boss) is more apt to have an interest in hearing about a person qualified in his or her particular specialty, may be planning to hire soon, hasn't processed the request through personnel yet, and can tell you firsthand what qualifications are needed.

As the process continues, you will:

- Make your calls, presenting your script in an animated, conversational tone with the flexibility to respond to questions.

- Determine the degree of interest and urgency. After developing some interest and establishing the fact that you know enough about the job to command the hiring official's respect, say that you work on a contingency fee basis, explain what that means and cite your fee structure briefly, stress that there is no obligation unless your candidate is hired, and say that you will mail a copy of your fee letter as confirmation.

- Get the job order details from the hiring official via the structured interview. Listen attentively to the description as presented, but guide the conversation to learn additional key points. Look out for unrealistic expectations, salary levels that are clearly not competitive, a protracted hiring period during which a lot of people have been interviewed but no one hired (there may be a reason), and situations where it looks likely that the position will be filled internally or by an ad. Make sure they are really interested in considering candidates from outside their city or region. If not, determine how much of a chance you have working in the limited area. It may be worth only a few calls.

The marketing cycle continues like this:

- If you find a good match for the candidate you are marketing, prepare a fact sheet (an abbreviated résumé) that will portray the person honestly, but in the best light for the position just described. That is not dishonest. One of your functions is to save the hiring official time by bringing to his or her attention only what is relevant. The fact sheet is sometimes used as a cover to a more detailed résumé provided by the candidate.

  It is a judgment call on your part whether the person's résumé adds enough to be worth including. If it is poorly written, or emphasizes things that overshadow that which is important for the job at hand, it may be best not to send it. On the other hand, a well prepared personal résumé can showcase the candidate's written communication skills, it can flesh out technical qualifications and performance data with which you are not completely conversant; and it can provide personal data that you cannot give. You will have to decide whether it adds more than it takes away. If so, include it.

- You must next decide whether you will profit sooner by continuing to market your current candidate or by switching to recruiting for the job that you just discovered. A number of factors will enter into your decision, including how convinced you are that the employer will really act to hire as soon as possible, your judgment of the chances of finding other strong candidates—considering the location, salary level, and so on—and the likelihood of the candidate's both meeting the need and accepting the job.
- Depending on what you have decided, either continue marketing to the list of prospective employers you initially created or switch to recruiting.

RECRUITING FOR THE CANDIDATE

Conducting a search involves recruiting a qualified candidate to fill a specific position. For these services, you will receive a fee from the company that hires the individual. Recruiting is the flip side of the marketing process just described. As you can see, there is essentially the same kind of activity required on your part, but with a different objective. Instead of finding a job for a person, you are finding a person for a job.

There is overlap; and as your sophistication in dealing with these people increases, you will pick up job order leads while you are looking for people. For example, "We would like to find a person like that ourselves!" is not an unusual comment to hear when you are presenting your recruitment script to a professional in the field. While not being able to help you by suggesting any candidates, he or she might be interested in hearing more about those you eventually do identify. As you become comfortable with your calling and don't see a potential disaster behind every unexpected response, you will learn to let people talk while you guide the conversation toward your dual objectives of identifying salable candidates and jobs; it all blends together and perpetuates itself.

In terms of the actual process, here is exactly what you do:

- Learn the necessary facts about a definite job opportunity from your structured interview with a hiring official, a personnel officer, or both.

- Prepare a recruiting script that introduces you and your purpose to the person called briefly (one minute or less), but thoroughly, and stresses the characteristics that are likely to elicit interest from the prospective candidate.

- Have a more detailed job order at hand in case you are asked for more information than you have presented.

- Prepare a list of likely prospects to call who might reasonably have an interest in the kind of professional opportunity you intend to present. As mentioned previously, your search will go more smoothly if you have a good directory or have been working long enough to know your contacts. If not, you will have to work your way to the appropriate person.

In every case you will be seeking assistance rather than directly recruiting a person from a company. There are problems with the more forthright headhunter approach to recruitment. If not outrightly illegal, it certainly puts you at odds with the people you are calling. The better approach by far—and the point of view that you must adopt—is that you have identified a really exciting professional opportunity and someone out there in the field knows of just the right person who is ready for such a career step.

That is the advice you are seeking. If you reach the head of a division and have a candid conversation with her, you are giving her an opportunity to suggest someone, rather than trying to steal her people. If she suggests that you are in there to take her people, you can comfortably make an honest response: "Joan, if that is what I were up to, why would I be talking with you?"

The recruiting cycle continues:

- Make your calls, present your script in an interested, conversational tone with the flexibility to respond to questions. It is entirely possible that the person you reach for advice about professional peers elsewhere is in fact interested personally. Be careful, but positive; and allow that interest to be expressed. It usually starts with some questions regarding the level of the position, location, salary, and so on. Sometimes these are just honest questions to help them help you. Other times they lead to an expression of personal interest. Use your judgment.

- Determine the degree of interest and urgency. After developing some interest and establishing your credibility by displaying knowledge about the specialty, say that all fees are paid by the employer and there is no charge to the candidate for your services. Establish that you work privately, professionally, and in a very confidential manner. The candidate needs assurance that he or she will not be risking embarrassment or possible job loss because of your efforts to reveal this, and possibly other, opportunities.

  Make it clear that you will present his or her qualifications in a general way that will not identify his or her name or company. When interest is shown by an employer, you will contact the candidate again, describe the particular opportunity and determine whether or not he or she wants to be considered. You will also confirm that there is no affiliation between his or her present company and the one interested in interviewing.

  You must avoid any risk of creating difficulty for candidates in their present jobs because you have them under consideration elsewhere. Some recruiters handle a search very openly, most very confidentially. You want your candidates to know that you will not be mass mailing their résumés or otherwise putting them at risk. To the contrary, you offer them a real service when you keep them in a position to be considered for outstanding opportunities without their having to apply or be identified until they determine they have a real interest. Responses to blind ads in the newspaper can lead to embarrassing situations for people.

A competent, professional recruiter can offer a nice alternative to the person who wants to shop around seriously without risk.

- Determine the candidate's credentials via the structured interview of the job application. Listen attentively, but guide the conversation to learn additional key points. Look out for unrealistic expectations, expected salary levels that are too high relative to present earnings (a 15-to-20 percent increase is a good rule-of-thumb), a history of job-hopping (a year or two in each position), personal circumstances that would make relocation unlikely (spouse has a great job or established business; child about to graduate, etc.). You want to establish clearly how this person measures up in the specific areas that were mentioned by the employer as important when you took the job order: years of experience at what levels of responsibility; measures of productivity and performance; number, size, and types of accounts handled; accomplishments; specializations, and so forth.

Continue the recruiting cycle as follows:

- If you find a good match for the job order in hand, prepare a fact sheet that will portray the person honestly, but in the best light for the position that was described to you. As mentioned previously, there is nothing dishonest about presenting only the applicable information. One of your functions is to save the hiring official time by bringing to his or her attention only what is relevant. The fact sheet can be used as a cover to a more detailed resume provided by the candidate. That depends on your judgment of whether or not the personal résumé adds enough to be worth including. If it is poorly written, or emphasizes things that overshadow that which is important for the job at hand, it may be best not to send it. On the other hand, a well prepared personal résumé can showcase the candidate's written communication skills; it can flesh out technical qualifications and performance data with which you are not completely conversant; and it can provide personal data that you cannot give. You will have to decide whether it adds more than it takes away. If so, include it.

- You must next decide whether you will profit sooner by continuing to recruit for your current job order or switch to marketing the candidate you just discovered. A number of factors guide your decision, including how convinced you are that this candidate will be likely to change positions readily if you find him or her a better opportunity and your judgment of the chances of finding a position that would inspire this candidate to make the move, considering the geographic and salary parameters involved.
- Depending on what you have decided, either continue recruiting to the list of prospective candidates that you initially created or switch to marketing the new candidate.

THE NEGOTIATION

Whether you are recruiting or marketing, things start to get really interesting—and promising—when an employer shows sufficient interest in a candidate to want to set up an interview. This will generally, but not always, begin with a telephone interview to determine whether or not there is potentially a good enough match to pursue in a face-to-face interview.

Your role throughout the process is to guide the relationship to the point of the two parties actually meeting and talking personally. This facilitates a great deal more that cannot be accomplished on paper or by a third party. It interjects the potential for the kind of favorable personal chemistry that can lead to overlooking a few formerly rigid technical qualifications this candidate may not posses. Granted, the reverse may be true as well. They may turn each other off. If so, it would have happened anyway; and you gain more by reaching this conclusion so you can move on to other business.

Your role in the interview process begins very early in your relationship with both the candidate and the hiring official.

When you take the initial job order, you want to establish the fact that candidates will be considered seriously and brought in for interviews, even if they are beyond the immediate city or region. Get that confirmed early, but understand that it can change. Sometimes a search that initially covers only a narrow region can expand out of necessity. Stay in touch to keep abreast of such changes. You will save yourself the frustration of generating good prospects who will never have a chance to interview.

On the candidate side of the proposition, establish immediately whether relocation is acceptable and if they will actually follow through if the right offer comes. Test the matter with them: Are they serious about considering a job outside of their city or region? If so, where and where not? If you get an employer interested but cannot deliver the candidate, you will have wasted several people's time and failed in your attempt to earn a fee. Again, the process is imperfect; and it is developmental in nature. Today's moderately flexible and interested candidate may be tomorrow's ready-to-go candidate. You have to appraise constantly each person's current status and operate from what you judge to be the actual position. Leave room for the person who might be tempted by the right offer: Keep him in mind, make him aware of appropriate opportunities, but don't dwell on him if he holds back in the face of a valid offer.

In terms of making the actual arrangements, your role will vary considerably. Some hiring officials will want to make the contact and the arrangements themselves. Some recruiters do not permit this and insist on being the intermediary. Others see that as unimportant, as long as they are kept informed. In all of this, you have an obligation to protect your candidate's confidentiality. Determine early on whether his or her situation at the office is private enough to accept a call from someone.

Many candidates have no problem with your calling and leaving a message. Use good sense, however; it would not be wise to leave a message to call the personnel director at such-n-such company or to call his executive recruiter. Also, leave no message if you are known reasonably well to others in the firm who might see a message left for the candidate and recognize your name or that of a local competitor's personnel officer or hiring official.

Discretion here is essential. Determine the guidelines, follow them strictly yourself, and make company interviewers aware of them as well. In some cases you want to call and talk only if the candidate answers personally. Determine the guidelines for each situation, and honor them strictly! One of the few ways you can encounter serious trouble in executive recruiting is by being responsible for someone losing his or her job as a result of the current employer's becoming aware of a job search.

After determining the telephone protocols for dealing with the candidate, the next steps are the interview and subsequent negotiations. Recruiters' opinions vary on how much preparation of the candidate is appropriate. It really depends on the candidate. If your practice deals with educated, sophisticated people it is important not to insult their intelligence. I mail an informational brochure or have a conversation that explains the recruitment cycle and some of what is likely to happen. I include a few tips on dos and don'ts for the interview. If you sense that you have a particularly nervous candidate or someone who really wants your advice—give it. If your candidate is a high-powered, mature executive with extensive hiring experience, your approach will be different.

The objective is to avoid surprises for everyone concerned. You will operate in almost every case, from a mental image of the candidate and the employer—you rarely meet either face-to-face. Like a blind person with enhanced nonvisual senses, you become a good judge of people met only on the telephone. It is your obligation to spell out the honest limitations that exist. If you know the candidate would not consider relocating for less than $60,000 per year and the employer is not about to pay more than $55,000, resolve the conflict or scrub the interview. There are many such points to which you will grow sensitive to the search develops. Stay positive and encourage working the problem.

If you present both sides honestly to each other and they still want to talk, fine. Never talk yourself out of a fee, but you will profit sooner if you avoid, or resolve, obvious potential conflicts. Given basic goodwill and mutual interests, almost any problem can be resolved. Your role is to identify problems early and solve them while they are small—before they are seen as attitude problems that alienate the two parties. It is rarely the problem itself that causes the loss of agreement in these kinds of cases; more often it is the perception of an undesired attitude—the way the problem is handled—that wrecks the deal. You can do wonders to prevent such impasses if you remain sensitive to the relationship and possible misunderstandings as they develop.

What I have just described is an objective, low-key version of closing. You can take a more formal sales-oriented approach to the process, if that is comfortable for you. The classic closes that you will read in the literature of selling have their place, but they are no substitute for getting the story straight from the beginning on what both parties want and are willing to do to get it. Then stay alert to adjustments in their positions as the process evolves. Finally, when they drift off into rigid postions that overlook other important factors, remind them what they originally told you was important. Work to persuade them to modify their stand where it might be reasonable to accommodate an otherwise highly desirable candidate.

Remember that you are dealing with three groups of human beings (or more): the candidate, which includes family and possibly a present employer with a counter offer; the client company, with more than one hiring official and probably a personnel officer; and the recruiter (you). It will always be the ages-old party game of saying one thing and having it come back via a dozen other people as a highly modified expression. Your job is to keep the ball in play and a constantly changing set of terms agreed to by everyone involved. In the final analysis, if the basic qualifications, experience, salary, and opportunity are right, the deal will close—assuming they don't scare each other off by reflecting unacceptable attitudes on the way to resolving the inevitable points of disagreement and misunderstanding.

THE OFFER, ACCEPTANCE, AND YOUR FEE

When all the calling has ended, all the interviews have been completed, an offer has been extended and accepted, it is time for you to be paid. When you took the job order you made the hiring official aware of your way of doing business. You explained that you are a contingency search executive recruiter and that there is no fee until your candidate is hired. You followed up by sending a copy of your fee letter that details the conditions under which you work.

As soon as the offer has been made and accepted—you may or may not be an intermediary in this process, depending on how the company chooses to operate—you will want to congratulate both parties and, almost as an aside, confirm that you will bill the company when the candidate begins his or her duties. On the first day of employment you will mail your invoice. Keep in mind that there is a probably a month in which your fee is subject to refund, if the employee leaves or is determined to be unsatisfactory. This is one of the fee letter clauses that is variable. The industry standard has been thirty days, although some employers will try to insist on a longer period during which you will refund their fee if the candidate leaves.

THE CYCLE

As I have illustrated, there is a constantly self-renewing cycle to the executive recruiting business. Once you have achieved your initial start up and have settled into doing business regularly, the only question regarding what you should be doing with your time and effort is whether you should be calling for the purpose of marketing a candidate or calling to recruit for a job opening.

It is virtually impossible to fully separate the two. As you talk with hiring officials in the field regarding a candidate you would like them to consider hiring, some of those calls will eventually lead to other job openings or additional candidates who would like to be considered for yet another type of opportunity. The same is true for your recruiting activities. You will be trying to call the level of person that you are seeking to recruit, because your candidate will most likely come from a peer referral; but you will end up talking with all sorts of professionals in the business.

By carefully structuring the conversation you will learn of other activity that represents potential business for you: They plan to hire in the future, perhaps at another level. They know of no one to suggest for the position you have described, but would like to hear of higher (or maybe lower) level positions themselves—and on it goes. You make notes, keep them for future reference, and act upon them when the time is right.

That correct time for action might be when you encounter a future situation that calls for such a person or job. The information gained previously can also present you with an opportunity to test the market for another kind of person or job. In such a situation you are acting on a valid expression of interest, not making a potentially illegal ruse call. As long as you remain active in your calling, there will never be a shortage of purposeful and potentially profitable work for you to do.

GETTING OUT OF AWKWARD SITUATIONS

You are operating an open and honest business that relies on a state of constant goodwill between you and the professional community in which you move. There is an unspoken understanding of what is going on among those with whom you will be dealing. You are finding candidates for other people's jobs and there is always the possibility that what you have to say will help the person you are calling or someone they know. With that being true, your call is almost always received with courtesy, but you must be sensitive to the fact that you are entering someone's busy day unannounced. Keep your call brief and to the point. Seek the information you need, pursue it if there is encouragement to do so, but be prepared to stay brief and thank them for their time if they either cannot spend any time with you or simply cannot be of assistance in a particular case.

There is always the remote possibility that your inquiry will be perceived as an unwanted intrusion, or even raiding. In practice, that reaction is almost nonexistent, if you are professional and careful when you deal with people. In those very few cases where your efforts to get some advice might meet with an abrupt rebuff ("I can't help you." "I don't give free advice." "I'm not interested." "No one here would be interested." "Talk with personnel."), take it in stride. There are a number of reasons that might happen from time-to-time:

- The person is having a bad day.
- They just lost someone to recruitment.
- They are truly too busy to talk with you now.
- They don't understand what you are doing.
- They don't want to be bothered.
- They see no benefit in talking with you.

There are ways around many of these situations; and, as your skills improve, you will apply techniques that will often open seemingly closed doors. When you reach that level of sophistication, by presenting your rebuttals in a brief, businesslike way, you will break down the resistance many times. Keep in mind that there will be those occasional situations when nothing will help. When that is the case, respond as politely and professionally as you can—for the sake of those who will call in the future, perhaps even you—but end the conversation and go on to the next call.

Remember that the next person you call will be totally unrelated to the last. Each call is new, and there is no connection beyond what you create in your own mind. One bad call should not make you timid about the next. Chances are the most helpful person in the world is only a call or two away from your low point of the day. This is a real attitude management business, and only *you* can control your thinking. What you anticipate in a call has a great deal to do with what you will find. Expect the worst and find it. Get enthusiastic about the great opportunity you are about to present and you will be surprised how much better your call will be received.

You will find that, given a chance and caught at a moment when they are not absorbed in some problem, people like to help. It is a compliment to most of them to be viewed by an outside consultant as someone sufficiently prominent in their field either to be considered attractive for a higher position or aware of those who would be. Learn your business well, so they can recognize quickly that they are talking to someone who knows the language of their specialty. Keep your conversation brief and to the point. Be sensitive to the problems of the moment and excuse yourself politely to lay the groundwork for future good relations, if that is what is needed.

TECHNIQUES AND RESOURCES

In the resources section of this book, there is a number of books and training programs that suggest specific techniques, scripts, and forms for dealing with almost anything that can happen to you on the telephone. They are worthwhile, and I encourage you to invest in some of them as your commitment to executive recruiting grows. As a minimum, I would suggest investing $10 in a set of basic scripts and forms available from RSE Marketing, Route 1, Box 435, Weyers Cave, VA 24486. You will receive a sample job order, candidate interview form, fee letter, invoice, candidate preparation handout, fact sheet, and scripts for both recruiting and marketing. They are easily modified to your own situation.

Many of the techniques are simply common sense presented in written form and applied to situations in this business. The same is true of closes that can be helpful in making clients react the way you want them to when decision time comes. You will have to decide where you fit on the continuum of people who operate in this business. They range from tough, hard-closing salespeople to rather genteel professionals who just try to arrange reasonable matches of jobs to people.

Arguments will always rage over which is most effective. There are days when a long effort falls apart and you come down on yourself for not pulling off some fancy sales close that would have saved the day (and a $15,000 fee!). There are others when you will be utterly convinced that it makes little difference what you do aside from gaining an accurate picture of who wants what, putting the parties in touch with each other, and trying to be certain that they communicate accurately. The answer is probably like everything else—you need a little bit of both techniques.

There is no shortage of how-to-be-a-successful-salesperson books at your corner bookstore. If you are not from a sales background and have not been exposed to the genuine virtues of the basic literature in the field, buy a few paperbacks and see what they have to say. One thing is certain: Executive recruiting *does* require you to present a product with professionalism and persistence in a competitive marketplace. Regardless of how you choose to view it, you will be using the techniques and facing the frustrations of a salesperson as you practice your profession. Don't be put off by the fact that some sales behavior will be necessary; adapt it to your personality and go for it! After all, you are just applying assertiveness techniques in a commercial setting.

One of the outstanding qualities of executive recruiting is that you do not have to spend time getting to and from appointments. Everything you do is on the phone, unless you decide to see clients personally for some reason. Think long and hard about that before you spend a lot of time on it. Your business success is generally based far more on the number of contacts efficiently made than on the fine points of evaluating someone's personality and appearance. Your time is better spent covering a larger part of the country looking for jobs and people than operating more personally in a local region. There may be good reasons why you are an exception, but base your thinking on that benchmark.

This telephone mode of operation puts you in an excellent position for dealing with awkward situations when and if they do develop. If all else fails, you can simply hang up the phone! There is never an excuse for a prolonged mistake or embarrassment. If you get out of control for some reason, hang up! When you are in the early stages of learning the business and need to look something up or consider which way to go, you can almost always beg off by saying that you have to take an urgent call and you will get right back to them. Always try to have enough presence of mind to make a smooth exit, but there is little lost if you simply hang up when you are getting nowhere anyway, or if it has developed into an unpleasant conversation for some reason. Few ways of doing business offer such an easy out.

Most of what you do will be grounded in your own positive perception of your work. It is absolutely essential to view your work this way. When you have such a frame of reference, it is easy to explain your activities when they are questioned. Or more likely, you will prevent the questions from arising by approaching people correctly in the first place.

Remember that you are either marketing or recruiting. When marketing, you are there to help the potential employers add people to their staff. The only basis for concern or potential for discord is that you may be interrupting a busy, high-level person. The answer to that problem is brevity. A properly presented script takes about 30 seconds and provides enough information for the person to judge whether they want more information or not, even when your call was unexpected.

If interested, they will ask some questions; and at that point you are operating in their interest. Sometimes they will say, "...Send me a résumé." That is generally unproductive, and you respond explaining that you are confidentially representing a currently employed professional person who would have to judge the merits of the opportunity before revealing his or her name.

That means the employer will have to be interested enough to give you at least the basics about the job and agree to pay your fee, if the person is hired. If the request for a résumé was just an attempt to brush you off, no further details will be forthcoming. Simply thank them for their time and offer to get back to them at a later date when their requirements might have firmed up to the point that you could get the information you would need in order to help them. Leave your name and number if you like, but keep in mind that few return calls will result. In this business you will have to initiate most of the activity.

Recruiting is a bit more sensitive. Your honest frame of mind must be that you are calling people in the field for advice about professional acquaintances who would be qualified for a given opportunity. A logical outcome is that the person called is looking for a change for some good reason or knows of someone who is. You are never calling into a particular shop to recruit their people! It is possible that the person you reach will identify someone who is interested or may even express a personal interest, but all of that is a byproduct of your fundamental search for advice.

Especially in this age of mergers, there is plenty of room for you to make inquiries regarding people who may be in a situation to welcome another opportunity. They either have been or soon will be merged out of a job! There are dozens of other reasons people consider a professional move: divorce, no room to move up where they are, missed a raise or promotion, want to work in a larger or smaller organization, personality conflicts, geographic preference, money, opportunity, and many more that will come to your attention over the years.

The most threatening situation in the recruiting environment is when you are not aware of the position of the person with whom you are speaking. If it is a foot soldier with whom you have spoken comfortably before, you can be candid. If it is an unknown, always go by the book. If you do not vary from that approach, there is almost no chance that you will face an awkward situation.

The worst case is that they just won't be able to help you. Worst of the worst cases is that they will accuse (most unlikely) you of calling there to raid that operation. Your answer is a very confident retort that you have called because of their excellent reputation in the profession and your belief that they might be aware of someone for whom the opportunity would be appropriate. As mentioned earlier, close with the comment that surely if you were raiding his shop you would not be talking with him!

A number of endings are then possible: They recognize that you have a good case, but still can't help you and say so; you part politely. They think about it a little more and suggest that you talk to some other people who may know of someone. They give the name of someone in house that they would not be sorry to see leave (in confidence, of course). They ask if you ever work with opportunities on their level and ask that you keep them in mind!

Approach your work with the right frame of mind and you will have few awkward situations with which to deal. It really is not a brutal business unless you choose to go crashing around recklessly. Your work pattern will be one of numerous brief conversations with people who do not object to a momentary interruption, but most of whom will be unable to help you in a particular situation. That is why you have to keep calling. It is a numbers game. Lots of calls will expose you to opportunities and people to fill them. Know what you are doing and be honest about it, and you will have few problems.

SAYING TOO MUCH OR TOO LITTLE

It is important that you learn to recognize the difference between a business and a social conversation. You are paying the telephone bill and using your valuable time. The people you are calling also value their time. There are ways to get the job done with a limited amount of conversation. You want to be polite, exchange a pleasantry or two, but get right down to business.

Most of your cold calls will involve verifying with whom you are speaking, that they are indeed in the business and worth your time, and then immediately presenting your 30-second script, without making it sound like one! Then the conversation will either end for lack of mutual interest, or go on. As it continues, you must concentrate on the business at hand and not the social aspects that may come into play.

Telephone professionals can be very impressive in how they move you through a structured conversation quickly, efficiently, and with a degree of warmth and charm. If it is a repeat call, they will reestablish the relationship by making a quick comment about you that only someone familiar with your circumstances would know (spouse's business, graduate degree progress, child's graduation, interest in managing money not people, a geographic preference, an accomplishment in an earlier job, etc.). After a minimum of polite but sincere social discourse, they will steer the conversation back to get what they need from you, but skillfully and pleasantly.

You must get answers to questions that you would not ask in a normal social conversation. If talking to a candidate for a position, you need to establish current salary and reason for leaving, the kinds of things that would be none of your business except for the fact that you are in a business that requires knowing. If you find it awkward to ask such things, you will have to overcome that; there is a good professional reason for you to pursue that level of questioning. If you are going to help the person advance to a better position, you have to know where he or she is coming from and establish that he or she is a good match for the job before you squander everyone's time and effort needlessly.

When you are cold calling, you will need to be ready to back off, but not too soon. You should usually persist beyond the point where you would end a normal conversation. There are several reasons. By asking a few well chosen questions, you can often get information that would not be volunteered. By prolonging the conversation just a bit, you can prompt thoughts and information that did not occur to the person during the first few minutes of your unexpected cold call. You give them a chance to warm up to you. It is a matter of judgment as to how far to go when applying these principles.

As tempting as it gets, do not get involved in lengthy

conversations that do not relate directly to making money for you. There are talkers in all lines of work. Learn early on how to extricate yourself from interesting, but otherwise unproductive, conversations.

SELECTING SITUATIONS WORTHY OF EFFORT

As you begin to build your contacts you will probably be anxious to deal with anyone. That will change as time goes by, your choices grow, and your level of sophistication increases. Your options will be at several levels.

The first is whether the hiring official agrees fully to the terms of your fee letter. The business operates on an honor code, and your agreement is legally enforceable if based on a well presented fee letter. You will encounter companies that will deal with you, but only if you agree to a lower fee—often 25 percent instead of 30 percent—or you will guarantee the placement for a longer period of time—sometimes for several months or even a year.

It is a free economy, and you own your own business. You choose to agree to terms that are acceptable to you. If you have no other business demanding your attention, or you have a candidate that can readily fill the position, a lower fee or a longer guarantee might make sense. The risk is that you will dilute the full-fee market for your services. If everyone can fill their needs at that rate, who will pay the regular fee? Usually you will be busy enough with full-fee business to politely refuse such conditions, wish them well, and look forward to doing business with them when they can afford your services.

The bottom line is that everyone gets what they pay for. If you work on the basis of a modified fee letter, it should be for a limited purpose and it definitely must assume a priority behind the level of attention reserved for your full-fee clients. You must be the judge in each case.

Other considerations when selecting potential associates in this business include recruiters who will want to split a fee with you. There are networks you can join that encourage such activity. Franchises tout this as one of their major services to you for the royalty you pay them. There is something to be said for the practice; however, it has a tendency to get cumbersome very quickly. Before long, even working with people you know and respect, you are trying to decide just whose business is whose (i.e. "That is my client. I have worked with them for years.") Do you accept a referral and agree to split the fee on just the placement at hand or forevermore—place the person a year from now in a totally unrelated job and still be honor bound to mail half the fee to the recruiter who provided the lead long ago?

Consider a specific and limited split-fee arrangement on rare occasions, but as a regular practice it is not the best thing to do. There are just too many ways for misunderstanding to develop and for you to limit your ability to deal with everyone freely. Look it over. It may be for you, but be clear on just what you are agreeing to. Also, be careful on client confidentiality for which you might eventually be liable. Not everyone in executive recruiting approaches it conservatively and professionally. If your actions result in your client's résumé being mass mailed by someone you don't control, you could be facing some serious problems. Know what you are getting into. If it seems to be a genuinely good deal and you have your client's approval to proceed, it can work out just fine.

Finally, the selection of whom to work with hinges on your judgment of how well the candidate or hiring official will work with you. The "send me a résumé" type of potential employer who will not discuss the job requirements seriously just is not worth your time. Be polite and offer to work with them in the future when they have a better defined need, but forget it for now.

The same is true of the candidates. If they don't have time or willingness to make clear their current status (to include compensation, responsibilities, etc.) there is no reason to waste your time. Be patient. You may just be dealing with a naïve person who doesn't understand your business; but if a reasonable effort to establish your credibility and the necessity to give you information leads nowhere, forget it.

With both hiring officials and candidates, you will have to establish the fact that you will be most respectful of their time and not bother them unnecessarily, but that it is absolutely essential for you to reach them to resolve important issues. The ability to communicate must be there! Do so briefly and in a totally businesslike manner. Let *them* suggest how they can do business with you.

Some employers want a quick call to screen the basic points on a prospect before you submit anything in writing. (This is often the case when it is a high priority, urgent hiring.) Others will want to have a fact sheet in front of them before they discuss it with you. Either is fine as long as you know the rules and can get meaningful feedback. As soon as you cannot get that, it is time to seriously consider getting off the project and back to the basics of either marketing or recruiting until you find someone who will do business in a serious way and with some sense of urgency.

A TYPICAL DAY

A typical day for you as a part-time executive recruiter will begin after you have had a normal day at your regular pursuits. If you are a college professor or an independent businessperson with flexible hours, your daily cycle may vary. You may recruit for a period of time in the morning and again in the late afternoon. If you are employed eight to five, you may have to consider working a city or region that is in another time zone. Depending on your location and your own lifestyle, your may choose to recruit for an hour or two before going to work, or after returning in the evening.

If you have an office situation that permits it, you may find it worthwhile to get a long-distance access code that you can use from the office and work for an hour or so from the comfort of your office, either at the beginning or end of the day (or both) while everyone else is out there stuck in rush-hour traffic. It will all depend very much on your own schedule, obligations, lifestyle, and energy level. If you really want to do it, you can find an hour to two a day, several days a week, to conduct a very professional executive recruiting practice as an executive moonlighter.

Everyone works a little bit differently, but most of your time will be spent on the telephone. That is the lifeline of this business. After you have done the research and made the exploratory calls to select your area of specialization and learn a little bit about the field, you must spend your time actively looking for candidates and job orders by using the recruiting and marketing strategies and techniques described earlier in this chapter.

You will spend some time preparing your calling lists—unless you can work well from a directory—by keeping track of when you have reached people, noting pertinent information for future contacts with the person or company, and so on. You will also have to spend some time preparing facts sheets and résumés when it comes time for such activity. All of this will depend on your circumstances. If you use a word processor at the office before or after work, that will dictate your hours. If you have a personal computer at home, you may want to handle it there.

As a person with limited time and energy and many other demands on you, you must set priorities and spend your time where there is the greatest potential for profit. With almost no exceptions, that will mean actively calling prospective candidates and employers following the cycles described in the marketing and recruiting sections here.

It may be tempting to structure elaborate database files of companies and candidates, read a lot of trade publications to really learn the business, and so on. That's nice, but it should remain clearly secondary to your obligations to contact people and identify immediate needs that you have a chance of acting upon and getting paid for. Define what hours you can make business calls to your specialty and do it. Do it then and do it exclusively for those hours. If you get the urge to read the literature, design the perfect file, or whatever, make yourself do it after the main calling hours on which your success will depend.

Depending upon your situation and the cycle in which you find yourself, it may be desirable to page your answering machine more frequently than at other times. On an average day when all of your activity is self-generated (as most of it surely will be), it is a good idea to check your machine for calls several times and return calls as necessary. That keeps you in business, makes you responsive, and occasionally puts you on to something that you can turn into profit. When you are actively presenting candidates, check more often. The hiring official may be calling for more information or to arrange an interview. You will want to return these calls right away.

None of this is difficult even if you are in meetings or across the country on a business trip. Buy an answering machine that lets you hang up if there are no messages, or enter a code and receive them if there are. A telephone credit card then lets you return the call. If you miss the person, explain that you are out of the office for a few hours on business and will get back to them; or leave a message for them to call you, if that can be arranged. Unless you are in an unusually rigid work environment, you should have no difficulty taking care of the few such calls that are necessary.

Most of what you do will involve your initiating the activity. Do not encourage return calls in your routine recruiting and marketing unless you can designate a time when you will be there to receive them. However, it is entirely possible, especially when marketing a candidate, to leave a brief message that identifies you as an executive recruiter and describes the candidate's qualifications in a few words, and asks the hiring official to give you a call if he or she would like more information. If they really are looking for someone, many times they will call and leave a message on your machine if you are not in. You can then call back, often to get a job order and possibly consideration for your candidate.

If the candidate you are marketing isn't right, describe

others or say that you will find the right person. If they have responded to your message, they probably have a valid hiring need and are worth pursuing.

Your typical day will not differ greatly from that of a full time executive recruiter. You will be designating hours of the day to devote without interruption to active telephone marketing or recruiting, leaving and receiving messages relating to your business activity, and doing the support tasks necessary to define future calls, submit current candidates, and bill clients for services rendered. The difference in your case it that the activity will be punctuated with other primary working responsibilities.

Stay honest with your primary employer. Don't bare your soul regarding exactly what is going on, but fairly separate your personal and company activities. Give your employer an honest effort; and, on those rare occasions when you have to make a call on behalf of your own business, do so quickly and discreetly. Chances are you will spend no more time on some quick checks of your answering machine and similar things than the average employee spends on personal calls and chores.

Discretion and fairness should be your bywords. Most employers would not mind the occasional after-hours use of a word processor or telephone as long as you are not using their supplies or running up charges on their account. In most cases, keep your executive moonlighter role to yourself and be sensitive to not giving anyone reason to resent your activities—or even know they are going on! Executive recruiting lends itself well to just such a low-profile mode of operation.

Chapter 5

Syndicator

I have always had a fascination with how people get started in any of a number of popular enterprises. Take your local fast food restaurants or motels along the interstate highways, for example. When you walk up to the counter or check-in desk, you are generally greeted by a plaque on the wall that says something to the effect that this establishment is owned and operated by the such-n-such group. Who are the faceless members of that group and how did they get together in the first place?

Unless you happened upon one of the large, sophisticated operations owned by an insurance firm or major holding company, you have probably just walked into a syndicate-owned business. Someone not very different from you saw the need for the service at that location, very carefully investigated the requirements for establishing it there and then formed a group of investors to put up the necessary money to acquire, build, and operate it.

Franchising is only one of many ways to start a business, but it is a very credible way of illustrating the cost of various kinds of start-up operations. An examination of these costs gives graphic proof that many relatively small enterprises are still well beyond the comfortable reach of an individual investor. Here is a list of popular franchise opportunities and their estimated financial requirements (McDermott, 1988):

- Baskin Robbins Ice Cream $115–140,000
- Benihana of Tokyo $400,000
- Domino's Pizza, Inc. $80–150,000
- Dunkin' Donuts of America, Inc. $49–59,000
- Econo Lodges of America $250,000–2,500,000
- Fantastic Sam's (hair-care salon) $78–140,000
- Jiffy Lube $185,000
- Kwik-Kopy Printing Centers $130,000
- Mail Boxes, Etc. USA $64–88,000
- McDonald's Corporation $200,000
- Midas International Corporation $138–155,000
- Nu-Dimensions Dental Centers $290,000
- Pearle Vision Centers, Inc. $31–66,000
- Physicians Weight Loss Centers $55–60,000
- Precision Tune $120–150,000
- Taylor Rental $287,000

Although prohibitive for an individual, many of these and similar propositions are well suited to syndication. There is ongoing opportunity here for the executive moonlighter. If you have the basic business sense and the ability to research and package a plausible deal, you can make the necessary inquiries and presentations to acquire and operate a major franchise—or other business of your choice. The services of a syndicator are needed, and there is nothing about the process that prevents you from doing it while holding down an ambitious full-time position with your primary employer.

As a moonlighting syndicator you will:
- Select business opportunities worthy of development.
- Research each business critically and establish credible grounds for its success and potential profitability.
- Write a business plan that demonstrates what you intend to accomplish, what it will cost, how you intend to do it, and what the costs and revenues are expected to be.
- Seek the objective review of experts in the business specialty and of prudent legal and financial advisors.
- Within the limitations of state and federal securities laws, prepare an offering with which to market the propostion to the potential investors who will form your syndicate.
- Act as the general partner responsible for the implementation of the business plan.
- Serve as the manager of the business or hire someone qualified to perform that task and assist them in developing the business.
- Inform the syndicate members of the progress of the project and seek their guidance appropriately.
- Retain and work with the necessary legal, accounting, and financial advisors to meet all legal obligations of the syndicate.
- Upon formation of the syndicate, receive reimbursement for your initial planning efforts and associated expenses.
- Collect appropriate fee for your continuing role in the management of the project as well as your share of operating profits and equity.
- Renew the cycle with another business idea.

Figure 2: An Overview of Syndication

If you do not have the several hundred thousand dollars needed to launch even a relatively small business, or are not interested in risking it if you do have it, then consider becoming the syndicator for the venture. It will certainly take time, effort, and even the initial investment of a few thousand dollars in professional fees and supporting materials, but if you want to do it, it can be done without serious disruption to your present life and work.

Syndication is a moonlighting venture that builds on itself. Success begets success, whether it is taking a local franchise and going regional, or simply branching out into different kinds of businesses in one community. With each successful start up come the confidence, track record, and contacts to go on to the next. Much of the effort becomes boilerplate for the next proposal, and it gets easier with each iteration.

Before I overemphasize franchising, let me make it clear that group investment via syndication is possible for almost anything you can think of in the way of a business venture. Your tastes may run to the real estate sector, which is rich with possibilities for reasonably passive joint investments. The currently popular bed & breakfast inn movement is another that combines potential for historic restoration, real estate appreciation, and an operating business. A lot of people can see the benefits to accrue from such a venture in their community. Your role is to run the numbers and come up with a thoroughly researched presentation. Make it convincing and credible by backing your opinions with expert consultation that shows how your proposal can be implemented profitably.

Another myth that I should dispel is that you, the syndicator, have to be the manager of the business—the guy or gal who gets behind the counter and sees to it that the team of burger flippers is running smoothly. You may choose to assume the manager role as well, but that is certainly not a requirement. In many instances it is probably an unwise limitation to place on yourself. If you are good at syndication, your time and effort will be better spent structuring more deals. Managers can be hired, and their guidance and supervision can be shared by you and, in the case of a good franchise, by its field support team.

Part of the secret of successful syndication is the appropriate use of professional services. It must be a profitable venture to attract and sustain a group of investors. The basic proposal must be very realistic and leave plenty of room for buying, as legitimate business expenses, the services necessary to form and operate the enterprise. With that honestly done, there is no reason you as the syndicator or any of your investors ever really have to roll up their sleeves in the business itself.

In order to attract investors to your syndicate, you must establish and maintain credibility. That might come from your present position if you are viewed as a person who, by virtue of what you have already done in your regular work, should know how to package a deal and see it through to successful operation.

If you have no such record, credibility can be established by starting out in some relatively small venture that will not require a heavy track record to gain backers; do it well and it will provide references and a showcase for the next bigger effort. Another approach is to associate yourself with a person who is successful in the field already—the owner of a small restaurant, perhaps, whose reputation is known and who is ready to launch the establishment of his dreams. He lacks the resources, but is willing to share the risk and profit with a group of investors. You, the syndicator, package the deal and derive much of your credibility by association.

An executive moonlighter is particularly suited to leading a syndication effort for another series of important reasons. High among them are the skills and attributes that have put you where you are today. You know how to speak to people and present yourself in a businesslike way. You have the ability to analyze a concept and outline the steps to be followed in putting it together. You can relate those findings to your potential investors. The professionals whose expertise you need—legal and financial advisors—are the kind of people you know how to approach and use effectively. All of these things, including the quality of the professionals you have used to frame the proposition, have a heavy bearing on the credibility of your presentation when it comes time for investors to write their checks.

One of the nice parts about syndication is certainly the fact that you facilitate the realization of a number of people's dreams. Your investors make money and share in the pride of association with a positive addition to the community. The principal manager or operator of the business—if it is one of those situations where the venture is based on launching someone with great talent but insufficient means—gets to bring his or her idea to fruition. He or she can even aspire to buying the entire business back as the investors fulfill their aspirations and take their profits.

What is in it for you? For all of the work and no money down—unless you have elected to buy a few of the start-up shares—you will earn a substantial fee for your services in arranging the deal, receive reimbursement for your legitimate out-of-pocket expenses (taken from the initial pool of investment money), plus retain a share of ownership and future operating profits.

The numbers will vary with the profitability of the venture. The first rule for most syndications is to insure a reasonable return to the investors before you take more than expenses for yourself. In a well conceived venture, it would not be unreasonable for you to recoup all of your start-up fees to professionals and similar up-front expenses. It is also customary for you to take from the initial pool of capital an administrative fee of 2 or 3 percent of the total capital raised for your efforts in packaging the deal. The remainder of your compensation will be contingent on the performance of the deal.

If there is plenty of projected profit to attract investors—enough to answer the question of why they should place their money in your project with its risks of failure when they can earn a guaranteed, if modest, return with a traditional investment vehicle—you can command a 10- to 30-percent (or more) share of what is left after their return is paid. The actual numbers will be determined by the venture itself. It can be structured so that your seemingly generous share comes only after your investors are already doing well. The potential for profit to you is not difficult to estimate: Arranging a modest $200,000 investment in property or a small business should net you a $4000 to $6000 fee for your trouble. If you have commanded only a 10 percent share in the value of the venture itself, you can expect another $20,000 after it has returned the original investors' capital and been sold for at least its initial value. This example doesn't attempt to attach a dollar value to your share of operating profits above debt retirement. It does not calculate possible depreciation or other tax benefits that may accrue.

There is no quick and painless road to riches; and syndication is not being presented in that light. All that I am trying to establish with you is the fact that the basic, crude figures just discussed—even when refined by a sharp-penciled accountant—leave room for a very fair and worthwhile profit for a moonlighting executive with the will to conceive, investigate, package, and implement an investment for syndication.

Be cautious. Be realistic. Let your first efforts be devoted to some very honest number running that shows you what can and cannot be. When it shows a rate of return for yourself and your prospective participants that offers no more than a certificate of deposit at the local savings institution, by all means opt for safety and forget the deal. With persistence you will find highly profitable situations that far outclass the government bonds that may be your competition at the low end of the scale.

The ultimate attraction for you and your investors is the open-ended nature of propositions which, if well conceived, should offer the prospect for big returns if things go even better than prudently projected. That is the excitement that you will savor, and it is the element of gamesmanship that will attract many of your investors who are looking for the thrill of participation and the possibility of picking a new winner as much as they are concerned with filling their bank accounts.

Why is such an opportunity available? It sounds too easy! Why isn't everyone doing it? These questions are asked of almost any money-making scheme. The answers are no more complex than a look within yourself, your family, and your circle of friends. People just do not take the trouble. They are too busy with what they are already doing. They assume that sizeable investments are all controlled by mysterious people unlike them and their acquaintances—and so on.

The opportunity is available because there is a need that has not been acted upon. It doesn't matter how many people think it is a good idea and have said so. Unless you are in the midst of a very unusual group, it will never go beyond the talking stage unless someone forces the issue by doing the necessary work up and presenting it. That is where you come in as the syndicator. You will certainly earn your fee and future share of the venture, and it would probably have never come to be without your efforts. All of the people who will benefit from the service, earn wages in its employ, or profit from it as an investment owe you. You, the syndicator, take it from the daydream to the reality. You make it possible for others to act by your planning and arranging every last detail in such a convincing way that they are attracted to it as a reasonable risk investment. That is why the opportunity exists, and that is why you deserve to earn a substantial hunk of money for your role.

Operating in the executive moonlighter mode, you can take your time in approaching a particular project. The key to making money in anything is in coming up with the right idea for the time and the situation. As you function every week in your professional life, you have the advantage of being exposed to an endless procession of ideas as you go to and from work and appointments. If you travel to other parts of the country, you have the opportunity to see things that are already working in other places that might well be implemented in your own community. Sitting on airplanes, in restaurants and conferences, you see and hear things that either already are or should be operating in the business services segment of the economy. Why not package one and present it to investors in your area? If the idea is a good one, you will eventually see it there anyway. Why not be the one to lead it and hold a percentage of it as it grows into profitability?

Your main personal investment will be time. It will be necessary for you to explore the idea thoroughly: See what is involved, what it costs to get started, how long it takes to reach the income-producing stage, the availability and cost of employees and managers, local zoning and other restrictions that might have to be overcome, resistance by other business, competition, the existence of plans by others to do the same thing, and on and on. It is quite a job to do it well; but it is anything but impossible, and it can be done without leaving your present position.

When you have as much information as you can practically gather locally and are convinced that it is worth exploring further, it will be time to get on the telephone and start making contacts in the industry. If it is a franchise, this task will be minimized by the work already done by the franchisor who will recommend—if not require—the use of certain equipment, supplies, and operating procedures. On your own, this job will fall to you and the route to the answers you need may be as short as contacts that you are already aware of or as long as a bunch of cold calls to likely players that you identify in the business reference section of your local library.

One thing does lead to another and, unless you are indeed starting something totally new (an unlikely event), you will soon have a list of people to talk with who will refer you to others until the whole picture comes into focus. The advantage of beginning with a good national franchise becomes more obvious as you get deeper into the process of inventing your own wheel. Another alternative for information on a large number of businesses is investing in publications such as those marketed by *Entrepreneur* or others mentioned in Chapter 14 who have done the legwork on what makes a certain kind of business tick. Still other sources of contacts and reference materials are national trade associations that cater to individuals in the industry or those who supply materials and services to it.

You have determined just what idea you are going to pursue. You have made a cursory study of the market and found that there are no insurmountable obstacles to stop you. A crude examination of costs and return shows that there is potential to make money. The next step is to begin preparing a presentation that will convince others that your idea is as good as you think it is.

Among the first opinions that you should seek are those of an attorney and an accountant. It is okay to take their conservative views of the venture itself with a grain of salt, but you should respect and follow their advice on its legality and regulatory and tax considerations. Depending on your state of residence, you will be facing some laws designed to keep hustlers from presenting hot propositions to the public and running away with their money. Almost certainly, there will be restrictions on who your investors can and cannot be; generally the regulations limit you to people who can afford to lose their investment if things go wrong without wrecking their lives and to those who should have some ability to judge the worthiness of your proposition and the degree of risk involved. Other restrictions that are common include restrictions on the number of investors and how you find them. Visit the local library to research the state codes that govern partnerships and the like. The ultimate problem for the syndicator is trying to put a deal together that requires registration under state and federal securities laws. To avoid this, stick to less severely regulated ventures.

It is not difficult or expensive to determine the legal and ethical parameters within which you must operate. The least costly way is to do your own homework in the library, then go to your professional advisors to verify your understanding of what you have discovered and the pitfalls to be avoided. But neither this nor any other self-help book, or even your own extensive research, should ever be substituted for sound and appropriate professional advice. Do not proceed until you have it.

With those precautions duly noted, I want to affirm enthusiastically that there is no reason whatsoever to hold back on developing and implementing your ideas. Keep in mind that different people will be attracted to your venture for different reasons. Some will barely qualify financially and will be seeking the kind of participation and money-making potential that they cannot achieve with other investment vehicles. That is fine if they indeed meet your minimum participating requirements and have been clearly informed that any such investment carries with it an element of risk. Turn them down if you are uneasy about their situation and their ability to sit back and let you run the project free of their limitations.

What you want to attract are investors of sufficient means to put up their money and let it ride with the understanding that they and their financial advisors have examined what you are planning to implement and are prepared to let you do it, so long as you act responsibly. The opposite end of the underqualified investor is the overqualified one who expects you to operate like General Motors or let him do it for you. It will be necessary to limit the shares of such individuals to prevent their having undue influence and control. You are the expert and the person who bears very real legal and moral obligations to deliver as promised. You must protect your right to do so.

Be conservative in your promises. The best approach by far is to promote realistically the money-making potential of the business you intend to operate. Don't sell it as a tax shelter. It may well be that there are tax advantages involved, but the Internal Revenue Service has become quite adept at identifying ventures whose tax savings are touted too loudly and whose potential returns appear to be exaggerated. Let your accountant assist you in the proper, limited phrasing of this aspect of the deal. The same tenet applies to appreciation of real assets. Investors should be attracted to the proposition primarily because of its apparent soundness as a basic business operation, not a tax or real estate speculation vehicle.

The moonlighting syndicator is often the kind of person who envisions deals, spends time scratching them out on the back of in-flight magazines or restaurant placemats, and, until now, has set them aside until that future day when there is more time and money to implement them. Wait no longer! This is not a get-rich-quick con by some guy writing a book. Use the enthusiasm you might normally expend on describing the idea to a spouse, relative, or friend to investigate the prospect of actually forming a syndicate now.

Play from your strength. You have the idea. Investigating it is begun by spending an evening or two at the library. If you have not done so recently, rediscover the wealth of information available in the business reference section of a good local library. There are guides to virtually everything—who makes what, who owns whom, associations and directories for everything under the sun. One leads to another; they all list telephone numbers. One of the skills you absolutely must develop is how to call an unfamiliar business or organization and persist until you reach someone who knows and cares about what you are doing.

Do your basic research and reading and it won't be long until you are somewhat of a local authority on the subject that you have chosen. If you have tried, you have also talked with people around the region and the country who share your enthusiasm about the topic and are feeding you full of ideas about where to go next with all of your dreams and energy. Package the deal. Be excruciatingly honest with yourself; and if the potential for a good return on investment is there, go for it. Investors will not be a problem if you have done your homework.

If you are going to remain a moonlighter and a reasonably passive participant in the venture yourself, as you probably should unless it is in your field and you really are trying to head out on your own, you must determine that competent, committed management is available for your venture. Plan to share your profit and incentive with that manager. Try to attract someone with a track record in the same or a parallel industry and who will command the respect of your investors. Provide incentive for the manager by making him or her a financial partner, if possible. You want them to sink or swim right along with you.

When your first scenario has played itself through, you will have gone light years beyond your old practice of having a burst of genius followed by frustration and inaction. See one of your good ideas become reality, and you will discover the difference between being a thinker and a doer. If money has been your only excuse, it is no longer a good one. If having to give up the security of your present position was the problem, that too is now solved. You now stand eyeball to eyeball with the toughest obstacle of all: your own inability to act. It sounds simple; but when all the obstacles have been removed for most of us, there is always one more (and the hardest of all to conquer): our own inaction.

If you can carve out a few hours a week from your work and family life, you can try your wings in a very serious way as an executive moonlighting syndicator. With a great idea of your own, you can start from scratch, package the deal, and keep a hunk of it for doing so. Should you want to start with something less ambitious, syndication can be applied to something as simple as the acquisition of a single family rental property by a group of acquaintances, or a proven franchise that has yet to reach your town, or capital to buy an airplane and lease it to the local airport's flying school, or a piece of equipment for a local professional person or business. The possibilities are truly endless. Stay within the bounds of regulatory propriety in attracting your investors. Enlist the services of competent professionals experienced in similar ventures, and pay for it out of start-up cost reimbursement. Structure a fair profit for everyone involved, and build in a healthy downstream payback for yourself. No one will resent it, and you will have prospects waiting in line for your next scheme.

Chapter 6

Money Broker

As an executive moonlighter, you bring many talents to the marketplace that you might not consciously recognize as having any unique value. One of these is your ease and comfort with following procedures and presenting information in standardized ways. Not everyone is so experienced, and therein lies another potential for profit in your after hours.

An area in which you almost certainly have functioned both personally and professionally is that of borrowing money. It is a field of enduring interest, one that has a way of intimidating many people—and not just the little folks applying for their first credit card or automobile loan. There is plenty of ill-at-ease feeling left over for the serious business borrower seeking start-up, inventory, expansion, operating, or other legitimate kinds of credit.

The world of money lending has an aura of mystery about it that is largely unjustified. When you come right down to it, it operates on some pretty straightforward and easily applied rules of credit worthiness. When you know them, you are capable of applying them directly on behalf of clients and sparing them the discomfort of being turned down. Better yet, while remaining totally honest and ethical, you can aid clients in catering to the rules. As a money broker versed in the tricks of the trade, you can operate in the interests of both the borrower and the lending institution. Through your good offices—and awareness of the bottom-line needs of both parties—a deal can often be arranged that never would have materialized had it not been for your intervention.

Most lenders do not bend over backwards to help borrowers portray their strengths on the lender's forms; and, conversely, most borrowers lack the sophistication to know what to alter in their request to make it fit the pattern that the loan officer has to see in order to present it comfortably to his superiors and, ultimately, the lending committee—the same folks who will likely pass on his promotion and pay raises.

This is a consultation business that you are completely capable of pursing while fully employed in another capacity. By virtue of its essentially confidential nature, it would take real effort on your part for it to surface as a matter of concern with your employer; unless you are now a lender or someone closely associated with the industry.

What you bring to the business is a number of attributes that your clients may lack:

- You are an institutional player comfortable in diagnosing the power structure of large organizations; you can figure out with whom you should be dealing.

- You have a baseline of experience in calling, visiting with, and making presentations to the very kinds of people who are encountered in securing substantial loans.

- You have the ability to be an objective third party in an otherwise tense situation.

The lender will come to trust your judgment and welcome your referrals because you have prescreened the clients for him or her. The paperwork will be complete and accurate; the surprises and misunderstandings will be at a minimum.

As a moonlighting money broker you will:
- Locate individuals and businesses that need assistance in obtaining loans.
- Determine which lenders are willing to work with you as an independent broker representing your types of clients.
- Match the needs of your client borrower with the requirements of your lending sources.
- Counsel your client and objectively determine the needs, credit worthiness, and special considerations that should be conveyed.
- Prepare the loan application and supporting materials for presentation to the lending institution.
- Clarify any misunderstandings and assist your client in responding to requests for further information or in satisfying any additional conditions imposed by the lender.
- Assist your client in applying to additional lending sources if the initial effort is unsuccessful but the potential for eventual success remains.
- Exercise good business judgment in selecting clients who are realistically qualified to obtain the credit sought.
- When appropriate, assist in the preparation of the client's business plan and similar documents.
- Comply with any licensing laws that govern people in your position.
- Collect the appropriate fee for your services, which may include flat charges for the preparation of plans and applications or a percentage of the loan based upon a prenegotiated scale.
- Expand your base of clients and lending sources.

Figure 3: An Overview of Money Brokering

ESTABLISHING YOUR FEES

As in any business endeavor, you must be sensitive to local ethical and legal considerations that relate to your activities. Each state is a little bit different, and you should begin your venture as a money broker by checking the legal and regulatory ramifications governing your particular situation. In general, you are free to assist individuals in understanding the lending process, the sources of possible financing, and how to go about presenting their requests to the various lenders. For these services you are entitled to collect a fee.

The precise basis for your fee and how you collect it merit the most attention. In most cases, there is nothing wrong with charging a fee to provide information or to prepare the paperwork associated with a loan request. Watch for regulations that might require a real estate broker's license if the loan involves real estate. Another area of potential conflict is in the structuring of things like limited partnerships, which require attention to SEC regulations and their state counterparts—rules that cover disclosure, the number of investors, how they are contacted, whether you are raising funds across state lines, and so on.

As your business and sophistication grow, you will become thoroughly familiar with regulatory and legal limitations on your actions. At the outset, satisfy yourself that it is alright to charge a contingency fee that is a percentage of the loan. That is the simplest and most common form of compensation. Until you become established, it will probably be the way you will have to do business anyway. There is little room for anyone to be unhappy with an agreement that requires the securing of the loan before you charge or collect anything. Everyone is a winner.

The essential part of working with a contingency fee structure is scaling it to the size of the transaction. This too will be determined by what the market will bear, but it is really dictated by common sense. For a reasonably small loan (less than $25,000), a 5 percent fee would not be unreasonable. It is not uncommon to establish a minimum fee of $500, or whatever you determine is the least amount to warrant your efforts. This also serves as an automatic screening device for clients whose interests are best served by approaching a lender directly.

As the amount of the loan grows, your percentage of it should diminish. The difference in effort for a large versus a very large loan does not justify a proportionally larger fee, and the market simply will not support it. Experience and your investigation of what others are charging will ultimately determine how you scale your fees, but a reasonable standard would not be far from a scale that is in the 5-percent range for loans of $25,000 or less, 3 to 4 percent for the $50,000 to $100,000 range, and 1.5 to 2 percent as you move into the half-million to the million-dollar range. If you find yourself working with even larger loans, you will find that 1 percent and less will still yield substantial fees and probably be about what the market will bear.

Be willing to start at a very fair—never apologetically cheap—rate for your experience level. As you build contacts and gain confidence, your fees will find a natural level that is comfortable for you and the participating parties. Fees are never a secret and have a way of being largely self-regulating. In the beginning, work on building your business by reinvesting in directories and cultivating sources that suit the clients you find yourself serving.

UNDERSTANDING THE BUSINESS

Remember that one of your most marketable attributes is what you are: a person with considerable experience in the world of commerce who can learn the buzz words and nuances of another sector of the economy quickly and well. One of the quickest ways to learn the language of a new area of business is to page through its publications. A trip to the library will get you started. Look at the periodicals and journals. It may be worth going to the business section of a university library to do this, since the topic probably would be of little interest to the community at large. Textbooks are also available, but you really should not find it necessary to study the field. All that you need is the basic language and a feel for what is important.

Libraries are also full of directories that will lead you to professional associations whose business it is to foster the professional image of various specialties by publishing membership directories, codes of ethics, training materials, newsletters, and journals. In the field of lending the premier organization is Robert Morris Associates, The Philadelphia National Bank Building, Philadelphia, PA 19107 (215-665-2850).

They have all sorts of lending publications they will sell to you. The *Commercial Lending Newsletter*, for example, is available to nonmembers. The newsletter costs about $24 a year and is full of up-to-the-minute information on commercial lending and credit. It links you to their other publications and activities including training, studies, and how-to articles as well as information and services from nonbanking sources.

A more direct approach to the challenge of familiarizing yourself with the lending community is to call or visit a loan officer at a lending institution. There are many plausible reasons for wanting to know more about financing from a bank officer. Without stretching things very far, it is fair to say that you are a consultant working on a project that involves the lending area and that you need to do some research. Ask what publications the officer would consult if he or she were investigating various sources of funds for different types of loans.

Prepare your questions before you make the contact, and then be prepared to go with the flow of the conversation. Graciously accept the help, and compliment the person on his or her knowledge. Most people are glad to help if you have called at a time when they can comfortably talk; the boss or a client is not sitting across the desk or an annual report does not have to be completed by noon. In the case of those contacts who are not forthcoming, thank them anyway and try someone else. There are many people in the business who would be glad to share some of their knowledge with you. If they are not comfortable naming specific institutions, ask what guides and directories would be useful in identifying lenders in other areas and in other categories of institutions.

There is a number of sources of funds. They are divided along the lines of traditional and nontraditional lenders. Examples of traditional lenders include banks, savings and loan companies, and mortgage loan companies. Nontraditional lenders would include insurance companies, venture capital sources, pension funds, and any of a number of specialized lending organizations that may be a part of other large companies with excess capital on which they would like to earn high returns through direct lending.

The uniqueness of your moonlighting practice as a money broker will depend on your ability to locate and develop little known sources of funds for your clients. In all likelihood local banks will be less than enthusiastic about working with you at first because most view themselves as able to deal with their clients directly without your intervention. In time, they may change their attitudes as you quietly demonstrate that you can deliver qualified borrowers with impeccably prepared applications and supporting documents. In so doing, you make the loan officer's job easier.

As an executive moonlighter you have the luxury of approaching the business in a more exciting way. While you may encounter some turndowns, you are free to explore a wide-open field by researching the directories of the various industries and making contact with some of the more esoteric sources. In time you run an excellent chance of establishing a quiet, highly specialized contact that will lead to a mutually profitable and satisfying relationship. The essence of sustaining any harmonious business relationship is having both parties get what they want and need with minimum hassle and maximum return.

Keep in mind that large, sophisticated financial organizations are not out there soliciting part-time people who operate out of their dens at night for client referrals. As I have made clear through the executive moonlighter discussions, there is no reason to let that stop you, or even trouble others with a description of the exact nature of your operation. Take it from me: They rarely ask—if ever. What they respond to is a mature, businesslike approach in your calls, correspondence, and eventual presentation of clients. Once you establish such a relationship, cultivate it by appropriately regular, but never bothersome, contact. Always conduct business with the utmost professionalism. Follow up and follow through; it's all that's necessary to be accepted as a major league player.

One approach to the business is to pursue it locally and derive your fees largely by helping people understand their needs, communicate them, and target who they will approach for the needed funds. This is a consulting service for which you collect a fee for helping people sort out their requirements and present them in a businesslike fashion.

It does not take a lot of imagination to see that this practice can vary from relatively minor activity, consisting of preparing loan applications for local business owners to present to the bank around the corner, to the preparation of a sophisticated venture capital plan for a budding high-tech firm. Where you choose to enter the field is a personal decision. There is something to be said for the satisfaction of helping the little guy in your own backyard. It can also be the route to a steady and growing income from a potentially large population of such clients.

If you are more oriented toward packaging bigger deals, by all means go for it. You are in the unique position of not having to derive income from your business in regular increments. A big hit every now and then may be just fine in your circumstances. The excitement that comes from playing on this level may be important to you. It also has the potential for being very lucrative once you have established your reputation with both selected lenders and a certain stratum of small-to-medium-size businesses.

Remember that banks employ loan officers whose job it is to solicit and develop business. Along with other independent brokers, they are after the same clients that you are. Your competitive edge must be in your own unique combination of sources and professionalism. Like any independent broker in any field, you have the advantage of being able to place the loan with a number of institutions, which gives you an advantage over the local bankers. Your experience as a practicing manager and professional person will lend an atmosphere to your correspondence and business practices that will make other money brokers look like hustlers. It is up to you to create that special niche where your talents can thrive and be appreciated. The bottom line in this or any business service is delivering what is wanted by the various parties involved at a competitive price.

When it comes to cultivating sources of money, it will be necessary for you to do research and write letters. Follow-up telephone calls are very important as well; a letter can be discarded easily, but an actual conversation can separate you from the crowd and convey overtones of competence and professionalism that sway the decision in your favor. At the outset, it will be necessary for you to approach both clients and sources as a very professional salesperson. This is unavoidable. The reason the opportunity exists at all is the very nature of the business. It is not without some difficulty and psychic risk. You will be turned down many times along your way to establishing a nice set of workable contacts. It is a part of the game; expect to go through it as you get established.

As an executive moonlighter, you have a number of tremendous advantages over most people who drift into money brokerage. One of them may be your knowledge of a certain category of potential borrowers whose businesses you already know well from another perspective. Perhaps you are a marketing representative calling on a particular segment of the economy that includes small firms with periodic requirements for borrowed funds.

You are already ahead in most of the start-up categories. You know the directories and publications that serve this market. If you have moved to your present territory from a previous one, you have actual contacts outside your present area of prime employment activity that can be developed as clients of your moonlighting services. When it comes time to discuss their needs and articulate them to a lender, you speak with the knowledge and sensitivity of an insider.

There are many ways to exploit this kind of knowledge using skills you already possess or can develop over a period of time.

It is certainly nice to be able to spin off of your current professional activity; but when that is not possible, keep in mind how easy it is to apply your basic knowledge of how business is done, your skill in communicating in the commercial environment, and other wisdom borne of experience to a parallel or an entirely new field.

If you are comfortable with your present industry knowledge, but would find it inappropriate to exploit it locally while still representing your primary employer, consider extending your reach electronically. Part of the magic of our times that inspired the writing of this book was my own experience in reaching around the country by telephone as an executive recruiter in the financial industry.

You must open your thinking to whole new perspectives of time and distance. If your regular job limits you on either dimension, it is entirely possible that your reach can be extended to a similar group of businesspeople in another region of the country. Lending is sometimes best done with some detachment. It is not uncommon for a local businessperson to favor placing a loan outside the local area where his or her affairs are not known to social peers.

Consumer credit has long since departed the confines of the local bank, with credit card wars raging among institutions in every corner of the land. The same is true of credit unions, which now look very much like banks and for years have loaned money for automobiles and other big-ticket consumer items without regard to the client's proximity to the home office. This is all possible because of very effective national networks of credit bureaus and collection agencies that will act on behalf of the lender when appropriate.

A similar situation exists in the commercial sector. Large banks have officers whose specialty may be regional, national, or even international lending. An examination of one of the standard banking directories such as the *American Bank Directory* of Norcross, Georgia, will illustrate this. Their territory is anything but local.

The secret to your success in such an arena is specialization. You either have or will establish a familiarity with a segment of the economy that few others will focus on as intensively as you. Properly done, in a few months or years, you will have cultivated contacts and industry knowledge in your chosen specialty that cannot be rivaled by a large institution having to cover a much larger and more general market in order to prosper. Also, the regular turnover in bank personnel will contrast very unfavorably with your stability, once you have established it.

MAKING YOUR CONTACTS

Armed with this introduction to the money broker business, you must now begin the actual development of clients and sources. Here you are again blessed with the gift of time. Determine what you want to do, and begin at a comfortable pace. If you want to operate locally, there isn't a chamber of commerce in the country that wouldn't be glad to sell you a directory of its membership. One or two from your immediate area will get you started in contacting potential clients.

Identifying clients in a different geographical region or commercial sector can be accomplished the same way. Examine your chosen industry, and select a region that is desirable for your situation. For example, calling another time zone after regular working hours may be important to you. Other considerations might include whether or not your chosen area is sufficiently insulated from your employer's market to avoid conflicts of interest or the possibly embarrassing disclosure of your dual roles.

The other side of the coin is the identification of lending sources. If they are to be local, the sources will be rather obvious and you should proceed to make contact with the relevant people. Should you decide to play on another level, it will be necessary to select the organizations and develop the contacts within them. When in doubt, consult the *Directory of Directories* at the library and proceed from there with further research, correspondence, and telephone calls.

With the basic information in hand, make some telephone calls to confirm the appropriate point of contact, spelling of name, correct title, and so on for a letter of introduction. It is not necessary to speak with the person. A helpful secretary or assistant will tell you all you need to know, if you ask in the right way. The most honest and acceptable approach is to introduce yourself as a private consultant with an interest in a certain kind of activity, and say that you understand their company has an excellent reputation in that field. Identify your best contact and go from there. Write a good, reasonably brief letter of introduction and follow it with an articulate, businesslike telephone call.

With the ease that comes from being a daily player in the world of commerce in your regular job, you can proceed at your own pace to make contacts on both sides of the lending equation until you identify viable prospects to put together. With that done, use common sense, good business practices, and ethics to explore and define the need and how you can fulfill it as a money broker.

Conduct a preliminary interview with your client and get a feel for the situation. Call your lending source and convey a thumbnail sketch of what you would like to submit for further consideration. If you haven't done so already, clarify what the lender needs in terms of content and format of the loan application.

Do your work on a contingency basis. If you do it well, you will earn a nice fee. If it falls apart, try another source until it takes. Worst case: You have begun actually doing business and have learned a lot about how to proceed more effectively in the future.

As in any enterprise, money brokerage thrives on referrals and satisfied customers—on both sides of the equation. Businesspeople obviously talk to one another, and it will not be a secret that there is this thoroughly competent and effective person only a discreet phone call away who can show you how to frame a successful proposal for funding. The lender will welcome the business and take comfort in the fact that on his or her desk is an application from a prescreened referral, and it is presented in a usable format that doesn't require rewriting or detective work to ascertain the essentials.

Nothing is instant, easy, or free of problems and frustration in its development and growth. That will certainly be true of a money brokering business that you choose to initiate on an after-hours basis. However, it is a realistic segment of the business services economy in which you can establish yourself and profit to a point that is truly limited only by your willingness to persist and get better. Today's technology makes it fully possible for you to mine this rich lode while working full time for someone else.

The trick is to open your first door and then develop your contacts and skills until you move freely as a highly specialized authority within your field. All you need are the brains, ambition, and persistence to use the readily available research materials and communications technology that will let you gather and convey information anywhere by phone, fax, overnight delivery services, or whatever the situation demands. It can be done quite well as an executive moonlighter.

Chapter 7

Expert Consultant

Depending on just how broad you want to make the definition of consulting as the "sale of your personal expertise" in the marketplace, it may very well qualify as the world's oldest profession. We all have knowledge, skills, and personal attributes that will probably command a price from others if properly presented to the right people.

Its historic origins not withstanding, consulting is certainly a major component in any examination of modern business services. The 22nd Edition of the *Encyclopedia of Associations* lists more than one hundred organizations that are in business to advise the millions of people who are out there selling their advice and counsel to individuals and organizations in both the public and private sectors of the economy.

The sale of your expert opinion is one of the most direct ways to cash in on what you already know. It is not difficult to do, although it does require a busines-like approach that includes the realization that periodic high priced days do not necessarily a high income make. The key to survival in the consulting business is the *consistent* sale of your services. That is something that often takes time to build, and it is a major justification for considering the executive moonlighter approach to entering the business.

According to *Business Week* (Byrne, 1987), about two-thirds of the nation's several million consultants are in the profession on a part-time basis. That is consistent with my experience and the advice of many people with whom I have spoken who urge beginners to keep the overhead down and continue to benefit from both the regular income of their full-time positions and the invaluable business contacts who surface in the mainstream of professional life.

HOW TO FIND CONSULTING ASSIGNMENTS

You may very well be that type of good-hearted soul who has been serving as an unpaid consultant for years. Some people do this out of the necessity of avoiding a conflict of interest. It is never wise to place your main livelihood in jeopardy over an occasional fee. But there is usually an easy task to identify a market for your expertise that will present no such conflict. If you find that you are being asked for your specialized professional advice with any degree of frequency—or feel that you would be if you made yourself more openly available—consider the possibilities of doing just that without creating resentment at your place of work.

One approach to the problem is the dichotomy that often exists between the commercial and the private, or perhaps even professional, application of your skills. If, in your primary job, you use your technical know-how to solve a certain kind of problem for Fortune 500 companies, there may be no conflict in offering essentially the same services to prosperous individuals who may benefit from your talents when they are applied to their residences, investment portfolios, financial planning, recreational equipment—or whatever.

Similarly, what you do for your primary employer for middle-market corporations may very well be a highly market-

As a moonlighting expert consultant you will:
- Locate individuals and businesses who need assistance in solving problems that require your special skill or knowledge.
- Determine which clients are in a position to actually purchase your services in the manner and at the price that you can make them available in your moonlighting capacity.
- Survey available consulting services in your field and establish a fair fee basis for your practice.
- Define a market segment that will not present an overt conflict of interest with your primary employer.
- Resolve potential conflict-of-interest problems with your employer by candidly discussing your limited objectives.
- Make your availability known within the relevant group of potential users of your services.
- Discuss the client's needs and prepare a proposal detailing just how you will approach the problem, the report or product that will result from your efforts, and the anticipated expenses.
- Schedule your activities efficiently, making optimum use of telephone, fax, computerized databases, and other services.
- Present a professional written and oral summary of your findings and recommendations.
- Comply with any licensing laws and function in such a manner as not to violate them.
- Collect an appropriate fee for your services based on those prevailing in your industry, plus previously agreed to expenses.
- Expand your base of clients with further contacts and referrals.

Figure 4: An Overview of Expert Consultation

able consulting service to physicians or other prosperous individual practitioners who are not a part of large enough groups to be targeted by the major suppliers of certain services. With some effort and ingenuity on your part, you should be able to isolate a special market segment that either does not presently warrant the attention of the major suppliers, or simply has not yet come to their attention.

This approach is an excellent and an effective one for the executive moonlighter who is alert to what is going on in the world. Whatever your field, if you are working with a reasonably large firm, the chances are very good that there are remnants of business all around you that do not warrant your employer's commercial exploitation, but are perfect for a beginning part-time consultant like yourself. Usually, your target market will be sufficiently different from your employer's to present no obvious conflict: but if you are concerned, discuss it with your boss. The correct approach is to avoid sounding like a start-up consulting firm and budding competitor, but rather like a professional fascinated by a tangential challenge to which you intend to devote a little of your own time—largely for the satisfaction of meeting a challenge and broadening your experience.

In actual practice, more than one successful service company has gotten its start in pulling together the bits and pieces overlooked by the big guys and fashioning an attractive market for itself. I know of a corporate CPA who found it profitable to show small businesspeople how to keep their books and tax records. In the process of doing this, he learned what a burden payroll, withholding, and all of the associated reporting and recordkeeping was and started taking care of that too.

Today, this CPA owns a company that is a major provider of such services nationwide. Before he came along, where else could the small businessperson pick up an inexpensive bookkeeping log at a popular retailer and clip a coupon for a firm that, for a nominal charge, would issue checks, W-2s and everything needed to keep the government happy? They will do it for a one-person operation or the burgeoning enterprises that they sometimes become.

There are as many ways to begin in the consulting business as there are problems out there looking for a solution. For many people—you, perhaps—it just sort of starts one day when you are asked to lend your expertise to a project for a limited period of time and for a certain fee. One assignment leads to another, and you are on your way. Unless you are the exception, however, with a reputation and set of skills that simply draw more business than you can handle, it will be necessary to market your services constantly. In business, nothing comes to those who wait.

Generally speaking, it will be necessary to get the word out that you are available to perform certain tasks. There is a number of ways to do this, including word-of-mouth among your satisfied clients and their associates in the business or profession.

Advertising is gradually becoming an acceptable means for professional people to make their availability known, but it is expensive and often hard to target. It may also result in a profile that is inappropriately high for your moonlighting circumstances. These problems may be less intense if you restrict yourself to special sections of trade, technical, and professional journals that cater to your potential clients. You are already probably familiar with a number of them. A trip to the library and a few hours of researching references such as the *Standard Periodical Directory*, or the *Directory of Directories*, or the *Encyclopedia of Associations* should put you in touch with a number of sources.

It is not uncommon for professional and trade associations to offer consultant referral services. They can be located by calling or writing to the sources found in the publications noted previously. One example is the American Association of State Colleges and Universities (AASCU). It has recently put together what they are calling the AASCU Consultant Referral Service (CRS), which solicits applicants from the higher education community, major industries, and professional associations. An individual can request a listing in the CRS database, which is capable of flagging more than 80 areas of expertise and 50 different subject-matter disciplines.

Listings such as this one vary in cost depending on the sponsoring organization and, in AASCU's case, your degree of affiliation with their member institutions. An annual listing for an individual consultant ranges from $50 for an employee of a member institution, to $100 for other nonprofit organization employees, to $250 for a private-sector organization employee. The objective of this particular group is to provide a pool of expert opinion available for a fee to colleges and universities in the broad areas of academic programs, external relations, facilities planning, institutional administration, institutional development, personnel and program administration—just about anything.

Like most referral services, quality control is an essential aspect of their program. Consultants listed with CRS are evaluated, and those evaluations become an important part of qualifying consultants for future referrals. Two unsatisfactory evaluations expel a consultant from the CRS pool. To learn more about this particular group, write to: Consultant Referral Service, American Association of State Colleges and Universities, One Dupont Circle, Suite 700, Washington, DC 20036-1192, or call them at 202-293-7070.

The demand for expert services is truly international in scope, and there is no reason to restrict yourself to a particular locale. In addition to listings of the type just discussed, it is also possible to develop a viable consulting practice by using even more direct means.

The most straightforward of these is to get a directory of potential users from one of the relevant associations or a standard business directory from the local library and do some old-fashioned cold calling. It is a great way to test the market for your skills. You can present yourself openly as a consultant wanting to put your credentials before them or as a third party conducting a survey for the sort of information you want to know. Businesspeople are not unaccustomed to such contact and, as long as you are respectful of their time, will gladly share their insights and opinions. Expect anything from no interest to an invitation to come right over and get to work. Even a referral to a colleague in another firm who might be in need of your skills is a successful call.

Another, less direct, marketing method is to volunteer your expertise as a speaker to professional groups or a free-lance contributor to trade journals. Your knack for standing up before a group of people and telling them about your field will often lead to calls and walk-up inquiries as to your availability. Such speeches can be in professional settings or at more general civic type forums, depending on the kind of talents you are trying to showcase and the intended audience. Just let it be known that you are willing, and it is amazingly easy to get on national meeting panels within your profession. The same thing is true at local, regional, and even national meetings of your potential clients. Most groups have program chairs who are anxious to schedule a fresh face with something new to tell their members. You will generally not command a fee for this; your reward is the exposure to a potential market for your consulting skills.

Communities of any size have special interest organizations that can be identified. One that comes to mind is a group of real estate investors who meet monthly to share ideas and hear expert opinion that may lead them to a more profitable way of doing business. Members of those groups range from neophytes with just a gleam in their eye to the quiet little government worker who has been building up his rental property inventory for thirty years and could very well own the meeting facility. Your advice on legal aspects of property management, engineering as it relates to selecting a piece of property, credit analysis as done by major lenders—or maybe how to keep their records and do their billing on a personal computer—might be of interest and lead to some consulting assignments for you. There are surely such groups whose orientation would accommodate your interests and expertise.

One source not to be overlooked as you begin seeking business as a part-time consultant is other consultants. It is one of those businesses that often experiences the feast-or-famine syndrome. It is not uncommon to find someone who is already doing what you want to do and who, for the time being at least, has more business than he or she can handle and will share some referrals with you.

There are many possibilities in this area and you will just

have to decide what is most compatible with your personal goals. If you are growth oriented and do not object to working in association with someone, or several other people, this is how consulting firms begin. Pooling resources for the purpose of sharing office space and clerical assistance can be the beginning of a growing business—if that is what you want, and if you are sufficiently compatible with the other person to make it work.

The economy's largest purchaser of goods and services is the U.S. Government, making it a source worthy of investigation by any moonlighting consultant. You have the unique ability to sit back and wait for the right assignment to come along. The most reliable printed source of government opportunities is the *Commerce Business Daily*. It is available in libraries, or you can have it delivered to your door by first-class mail for $243 a year ($173 by second-class mail), or receive a six-month trial subscription for $122 and $87, respectively. The address is: Superintendent of Documents, Government Printing Office, Washington DC 20402-9371 or you can call 202-783-3238 with your Visa or MasterCard.

The banner across the front page of every issue—and yes, it is, as its name implies, *daily*—bills it as "A daily list of U.S. Government procurement invitations, contract awards, subcontracting leads, sales of surplus property and foreign business opportunities." That covers a lot of territory and many of the entries call for complex services that will only be delivered by huge defense contractors and the like. On the other hand, there are countless listings that hold potential for performance by individuals or small organizations with expertise in a broad spectrum of areas.

The only way to get a feel for the potential for exploiting the *Commerce Business Daily* is to examine actual copies of it over a period of time. It is published on newspaper-type stock and has all the readability of a major city classified ad section, but it is a gold mine for those who know how to use it. The section devoted to "Expert and Consultant Services" lists opportunities ranging from highly technical engineering matters to requests for historians to prepare studies of American Indian land and water rights in different parts of the country. The solicitations are not at all limited to Washington, DC, although the initial point of contact is frequently there.

Another useful application for the *Commerce Business Daily* for the moonlighting consultant is the section entitled "Contract Awards." By reading it under your areas of interest, it is possible to identify the companies that are *winning* government contracts. It will tell you the dollar value of the award and give you the name and address of the recipient. In many cases, it will be a major company whose name you recognize. In other instances, it will be the name of companies, especially in the greater Washington, DC area, that are known with varying degrees of affection as "beltway bandits," firms that maintain offices and limited permanent staff for the purposes of identifying and securing government contracts. They then scurry about and hire consultants to do much of the work. There is nothing illegal about this. Many are listed with government agencies and have the track records of successful performance essential in securing these multimillion-dollar contracts.

Your opportunity is to be found in contacting these otherwise obscure companies and letting them know of your availability, areas of expertise, and so forth. It is a very realistic way to enter a field that would otherwise be too sophisticated for you to approach as an individual. They are heavily concentrated in the Washington area, but the work that they contract to do is not. They may very well establish a relationship with you to fulfill an obligation of their contract in some far corner of the country or the world. Do not feel that you are imposing on them. It is very much a two-way street, with the contracting firms seeking permission to use *your* resume as a part of their proposals to gain future business.

This and other very viable options should not be overlooked because of the ambiguity that surrounds them. Those common cynical questions, such as, "If it is so darned easy, why isn't everyone doing it?" or "Why isn't the guy telling you about it rich?" reveal a common problem among those about to seek new opportunities. We are conditioned throughout life to fill out neat little applications for everything we do from applying to college to competing for a job. The franchise industry thrives because we are all very anxious to follow step-by-step procedures to reach a probable result. That is all fine, and it is one way to approach things—but it is not the only way.

If you are looking for a way to escape the shackles of conventional work and income—or merely to supplement it or test something different as an executive moonlighter—you may have to traverse some uncharted ground to find it. Remember that one of the advantages of your situation is license to hunt and probe and be selective in where and how you choose to apply your unique skills. A document as forbidding as the *Commerce Business Daily* may very well contain the name of a company that has just secured a major contract in your area of expertise that would just love to identify you as a part-time source of talent in fulfilling its newfound obligations.

A little bit of diligence in finding such a listing in all the chaff of the general publication can pay rich dividends. But not if you fail to persist in getting on the telephone (most public libraries have telephone books for major population centers; if yours does not, dial long-distance information) or into a directory and determining the name of a relevant contact within that firm. Get past the receptionist, and find your professional counterpart. If you are an engineer, a programmer, a technical writer, or whatever, probe until you are on the line and talking with that person. See if he or she needs your contribution and supply your resume immediately with a cover letter citing your telephone conversation and thanking them for their interest in you. It works!

HOW MUCH TO CHARGE

A topic of concern for everyone entering the consulting business is how to establish an appropriate fee structure. There is no pat answer to the question, and your best guidance is to be found in what others charge for similar services in your market.

According to *Business Week* (Byrne, 1987), most consultants charge between $500 and $800 a day plus expenses, while the superstars of the industry command as much as $5000 a day. Charge the going rate or slightly less, but never significantly less, as you seek to establish yourself. As a moonlighter you will learn that $500 a day sounds good, but averages out to a paltry per-hour rate for your total time invested unless many such days are billed to paying clients.

Whether your questions relate to fees or other aspects of the consulting business, this is a popular topic; so a trip to the library or bookstore will buy you a lot of advice. The *Entrepreneur* publishes a manual on the subject. It and others are listed in the information sources chapter of this book. A currently popular book on the subject is Robert Kelley's *Consulting: The Complete Guide to a Profitable Career*. It can be purchased at your bookstore or through the publisher.

The other sources for advice, publications, training, and contact with others working in your field are the associations cataloged in the *Encyclopedia of Associations* and similar publications. For example, the *Business Week* article quoted throughout this book mentions that the Institute of Management Consultants in New York has a highly regarded three-day "Fundamentals of Management Consulting" course that is available for less than $500. By availing yourself of such affiliations, publications, and sources of information, you can do a lot to shorten the learning curve that is part of becoming a successful consultant.

Now that we have explored the consulting business and delved into some of the ways that it might be approached as an executive moonlighter, let me end by encouraging you to sit back and look at the big picture. There are many ways to complicate something like consulting to the point where you will never give it a fair try. That really should not be necessary if you will just remember the fundamentals of the the consulting business and what justifies its continued existence.

With no exceptions that I can think of, consultants are engaged for one of three purposes: (1) They are selling a brand of expertise that is so specialized that it either does not exist broadly in the marketplace; (2) the purchaser of that expertise cannot justify a full-time member of its own staff in such a narrow specialty; or (3) the consultant represents an independent, unbiased, outside opinion that cannot be obtained in-house or from associated companies.

If you can fit your talents into one of the above categories and have the training, knowledge, and experience to command the respect of the marketplace, you stand an excellent chance of becoming a successful consultant. As a moonlighter, you are in the enviable situation of cautiously testing the demand for your expertise and nurturing it until you have targeted the segment that meets your needs and aspirations.

If full-time consulting is your ultimate goal, you can ease into it with your lessons learned and client base established in the comfort of the moonlighting environment. If your objective is no more complex than wanting to function as an authority in your field operating beyond the confines of your present position, consulting as a properly situated moonlighter can accomplish that as well. Such an arrangement can bolster your income and ego strength while it provides a degree of total career satisfaction that lets you remain a contented member of your primary employer's team. The executive moonlighter can choose the optimum combination of consulting and full-time employment.

Chapter 8

Professional Speaker

Some people are born public speakers. Others get forced onto the platform by the circumstances and demands of their jobs and then learn to love it. There is little difference between the speaker and an entertainer who experiences no more satisfying high than that of an appreciative audience. If you have learned to love public speaking, are good at it, and can develop and sustain a series of popular topics, you may find a lucrative market for your talents as an executive moonlighter.

THE CONTEMPORARY SPEAKER

In my conversations with the president of a major national speakers' bureau, I had reinforced one of the enduring truths of the marketplace: There are always too many available, but never enough good ones! That is as true for speakers and trainers as it is for any other product or service. Moonlighting is the norm for speakers. Few actually do it full time; and even those who do first honed their skills and built their reputations on the part-time circuit.

The term speaker needs some definition when it is used in the context of contemporary business services. There is actually a very well defined, functional, and economically justified place for speakers in business today. They are specialized consultants who make their pitch and apply their expertise to a lecture hall or dining room full of people rather than a boardroom full of top managers. Their task is to inform, to motivate, to train and to change human behavior by virtue of what they have to say and how they say it. In doing this they are also generally expected both to entertain and command the respect of their audiences.

If all of this sounds a lot like what you have been doing for a long time in your business or profession as you travel around the country making presentations on behalf of your employer, consider the possibility of changing your act and your audience and collecting a nice fee for the effort. There are several strata of professional speakers who fall somewhere below the big-name superstars and considerably above the local Rotary Club folks who struggle with the lunchtime nap crowd. You can identify your appropriate entry level and build your way up to any level that your talent and material will command, while still maintaining your present position. This business was *made* for the executive moonlighter.

I am always pleasantly surprised when I attend a meeting or workshop somewhere and find on the program a speaker that I have never heard of who not only keeps me awake but actually sends me home with my spirits lifted, my horizons broadened, and my creative juices pumping. If you have the gift and the motivation, there is room for you on that circuit.

As you have undoubtedly heard, the classic comedic response to the question, "How do I get to Carnegie Hall?" is "Practice, practice, practice!" In the public-speaking profession, the street map reads the same. It is always impressive to see a thoroughly practiced master moving and manipulating the audience at will and having the group love every minute of it. That is as true of an outstanding motivator before a group of plywood salesmen as it is with Lee Iacocca before Congress.

As a moonlighting professional speaker you will:
- Identify an area of your expertise that has sufficient popular appeal to command fees for group presentations.
- Candidly appraise your own speaking ability and do what is necessary to polish your skills to the competitive point.
- Use modern video technology to practice and perfect your performance in conjunction with professional criticism and assistance.
- Consider the impact of your speaking on your current primary employer and resolve any potential conflicts.
- Contact a national speakers' bureau and seek their earnest opinion on the appeal of your presentation and incorporate any suggestions for changes of emphasis.
- Make your availability known within the potential audience groups and begin building experience and a following.
- Determine your audience's characteristics, interests and situation before delivering your speech.
- Make effective use of telephone, fax, computerized databases, and other such services to keep your material current.
- When warranted by sufficient experience and demand, delegate the business aspects of marketing and scheduling your presentations to a professional speakers' bureau.
- Constantly appraise the marketplace and plan new material and markets for your services.
- Collect an appropriate fee for your services based on those prevailing in the industry, plus previously agreed-to expenses.
- Expand your base of clients with further contacts and referrals.

Figure 5: An Overview of Professional Speaking

YOU HAVE A HEAD START

A positive irony is that, as a moonlighting executive, you quite likely bring to the field many hours logged before the crowd. Depending on your profession, you almost certainly have spent a lot of time making group presentations, if not formal speeches to sit-down audiences. The effect is not that different; and the rough jewel that you may already be is probably not all that far from the commercial-grade speaker you may aspire to become, if you like that sort of thing—and you truly must to pursue it successfully.

If you love the thrill of getting the butterflies and then dismissing them as you are introduced and rise to command the head table for your designated time, this may be the business for you. Unlike many other forms of consultancy and executive moonlighting, a speaker can rather easily select an area of expertise that is considerably far removed from his or her everyday profession. Being an attorney who is also a platform authority on some obscure special field of knowledge—culture or humor, perhaps—is not that difficult or unusual. It is entirely possible to stick with your main line specialty, of course; but you are free to leave it behind or modify it to meet the needs of your audience.

Public speaking can be a passion not far removed from the performing arts. Video technology allows the serious student to practice before a video recorder and critique his own work endlessly as he evolves from worthy presenter to polished speaker. You can hire coaches to help you eliminate the dialect and grammar problems you never realized you had. In no time, your speaking voice will bear homogenized grammatical quality worthy of Henry Higgins, the evening news, or the telephone company's information computer.

GOING PROFESSIONAL

There are more conventional ways to gain experience and receive constructive criticism for your public-speaking efforts. Toastmasters International has been providing a forum for amateurs who want to practice and improve their platform skills since 1924. They have 125,000 members participating in 5800 local groups.

If you have advanced to the professional or semiprofessional speaker level, membership in the National Speakers Association (NSA), headquartered in Phoenix, Arizona might be more appropriate. It also has training programs to help the aspiring professional speaker. Its CSP (Certified Speaking Professional) designation is a recognized mark of professionalism in the speaking trade. While NSA is not a speakers' bureau, it has a special interest group consisting of providers of that service. Its other specialties represent the topics found most frequently in today's speakers' market: religion, health and fitness, humor, sales training, and the many topics covered by workshops and seminars.

One profitable pursuit for the executive moonlighter of sufficient stature is as an informative, stand-up speaker able to command fees at major meetings for the purposes of informing, motivating, and entertaining. While nothing is really beyond the realm of the talented presenter, there may be a better fit for most working professionals in the areas of sales training and workshops or seminars. It is in this area that you probably have gained your experience and can most easily adapt. These fields also relate more directly to the bottom line of the sponsoring organizations, so more opportunities abound for marketing your skills.

In selecting your specialty, keep in mind the perspective of those who will be hiring you. Your services must be either affordable or income-generating, you must have credibility in your subject area, and you must be able to adapt your presentation to the needs of their particular situation.

SPEAKER COMPENSATION

The fee consideration is a variable one; and it fluctuates with your competence and degree of celebrity within your field, if not as a national figure. The best known speakers today command $25,000 and more for a single presentation. The norm is closer to several thousand dollars for an experienced, but not superstar, after-dinner speaker.

At the time of this writing, Tom Peters, the management author and speaker, averages $23,000 per session. Buck Rogers, the retired captain of IBM, settles for a consistent $12,500. An excellent psychological presenter from California who has yet to establish a real name for himself is good for $2000. A highly regarded local businesswoman in the Washington area earns $1000 per engagement. The speaker's agency fee varies, too. The rule of thumb is 25 percent for a presentation fee of less than $5000, 20 percent for a higher fee, and a further declining percentage as the fee rises toward the superstar levels.

There are nonmonetary forms of compensation in this business, too. When you are in negotiations with a group to deliver training or a keynote speech at some desirable resort location, you may want to accept a reduced fee in consideration of a week of meals and accommodations for you and a companion. Both sides can win in such arrangements: The group has considerable power with the host facility when it comes to reduced rates for members of its party. The same is true of airfare, which is negotiated at group rates and could easily include your companion. And you basically are paying for a much needed vacation with tax-free dollars.

Compensation is really anything that is of value to you. If you are at the beginning of your speaking career, you may be able to profitably trade for your time on the podium such things as testimonials and references, videotapes of your presentation, and extra printed copies of the organization's program materials that highlight and showcase your talent. The testimonials and references establish you as a professional with a verifiable track record. Videotapes are used by you, and possibly by your coach or other respected associates, to critique your skills. It can do double duty as an audition tape. At many major conventions, the sponsoring group goes to considerable expense to hire professional video production companies, and you can negotiate a studio-quality record of your performance as part of your fee.

As an executive moonlighting speaker, you will be able to build a rather substantial set of credentials—and enjoy many beautiful places—if you are willing to trade extended accommodations and travel arrangements for part of your fee. In doing this you will make your services more attractive to the groups, and often this will influence their selection more than if you had approached them with a rigid fee or speakers' bureau contract. One disadvantage of the bureau's arrangement is that its share of your fee is often collected up front from the organization as an advance. If you do not have such a requirement, you may prevail when the decision is a close one. Assuming you really have something to offer and do your job well, each succeeding job will come easier based on your increased experience and an enhanced reputation.

Associating yourself with a speakers' bureau can have its advantages. If it is an established one with a solid reputation, you instantly share in its prestige and respectability. They vouch for your competence, which is a valuable asset early in your speaking career. In return for a percentage of your earnings, they handle all of the tasks that you may very well wish to avoid, such as promotion, scheduling, billing, and collecting the fee. They also have the resources to produce an acceptable substitute should you find it impossible to honor your speaking obligation.

Ethics are a critical part of this and any business service. For the traveling speaker or trainer, one issue that often presents itself is the question of prorated travel expenses when making more than one presentation on a particular trip. As anyone who has ever traveled on business can attest, you can rarely be paid too much for the aggravation and indirect expenses of dragging yourself through airports, hotels, restaurants, and rental car agencies for days at a time.

With that said, let me suggest that you offer some accommodation to your clients when significant economies accrue due to common scheduling. I do not believe it requires dollar-for-dollar reductions, but rather some adjustment that acknowledges the potential duplication of reimbursements and makes a good-will effort to be fair.

MARKETING YOUR TALENT

One of the best ways I know to portray the true potential of a moonlighting speaker's career is to describe a program that is established and working. I have selected a company that does its business in the seminar and training segment of the public-speaking industry. Their fees are relatively modest, but the opportunity for growth is tremendous. For that reason, I believe this example is more inspirational than my reciting a litany of famous people and the outrageous fees they command.

The firm whose program I will describe is the Boulder, Colorado-based CareerTrack Seminars, Incorporated. They produce over 2500 one-day training seminars a year in hundreds of cities in the United States, Canada, and Australia. They do it by attracting accomplished speakers who have something topical to say and the proven ability to do it with great skill and enthusiasm. The audiences targeted are individuals and groups who can benefit from the seminars' solutions to everyday life or business problems.

CareerTrack is representative of the kind of organization you may want to contact after you have become reasonably well established. They are not in the business of training seminar leaders, so they want irrefutable up-front evidence that you are already an accomplished presenter. Their rule of thumb is that if you are not yet comfortable making your pitch to groups of from 50 to 500 or more, you aren't ready for their program.

Speakers who are booking at least 30 paid speaking engagements a year would probably meet their minimum expectations, so you have some work to do as a moonlighter before approaching them. The good news is that a moonlighting executive will be able to compile just the kind of credentials that are being sought by the likes of CareerTrack.

What they want to see before even discussing anything with you is a five-hour videotape of you actually conducting a full-day seminar. In their opinion, if that sounds like an unreasonable requirement, you are not in their league and need to spend some more time in the trenches. They want to see a resume and a photo, but the proof of the pudding is how you handle a day before a paying audience.

If it is your goal to leave your present full-time position for a career of speaking or some combination of consulting, writing, and speaking, then a company like this can offer a nice transition. Their basic contract is for a minimum of 72 training days per year, averaging six per month. In consideration of that commitment, you will be paid $500 per day plus airfare, hotel, and $60 a day for incidental expenses.

They acknowledge that you are not going to get rich on their guaranteed $36,000 per year, but it does provide just the base that many speakers seek. There is the opportunity to book additional days, of course; and you can also arrange to present in-house programs for companies whose employees attended and liked the seminar and recommended it be presented to more staff members. You are also free from chores like promoting yourself, booking hotels, registering participants, and so on. Your job simply is to show up and make a terrific presentation.

By associating yourself with an organization like this, you also potentially benefit from their promotional efforts that may land you on some local—or perhaps national—television broadcasts. They have links to publishers that can produce your work in print or cassette formats, which will also generate income for them and for you.

Additional considerable profit potential exists for the speaker/consultant who is able to schedule other assignments around the contracted activity just discussed. It is expected that you will meet your obligations; beyond that you are on your own. Substantially higher fees can be commanded for your presentations booked outside these arrangements; and often, with proper scheduling, you save travel expenses by stopping off on your way to or from a paid engagement.

There are as many ways to work a private speaker business as there are people doing it and clients attracted to what you have to say. By citing the above illustration, I am providing you with a middle-of-the-road benchmark from which to fashion your own approach to participating in the business.

As has been stressed in earlier chapters, executive moonlighting is an ideal way to try something that you could never rationally plunge headlong into on a full-time basis. Public speaking on an international level would exist only as a fantasy for most working professionals with all of the obligations of an established lifestyle. However, using the vehicle of moonlighting, it is entirely possible to begin and advance your level of competence and talent to the point where you could make public speaking a full-time and very lucrative occupation.

As I have described, you can moonlight as a speaker, using a support network that permits the high degree of flexibility you need to experience the freedom you crave. With prudence, the executive moonlighting years will provide you with more than experience. It is entirely possible that the invested earnings from your after-hours endeavors will ultimately provide the financial safety net to ease your transition to a freer life. For others, the ongoing ego trip and extra income of a successful executive moonlighter speaking career will make staying in the traditional workplace an acceptable, even desirable alternative.

Chapter 9

Seminar and Trade Show Promoter

By now you probably have attended enough training seminars and trade shows to have thought that you could do the job better than the people in charge. Another common occurrence when sitting in a seminar is to have the person next to you lean over and discreetly share with you his pencil-pad estimate of the headcount in the room multiplied by the fee paid. The obvious conclusion is that someone is making a lot of money that day.

One exercise I can recommend to you is just to collect your office mail relating to seminars and workshops for several weeks at the right time of the year, and you will have a pretty good overview of the industry. Doing this will show you what is selling, where, and for how much. Another revelation is that the sponsoring companies are not at all confined to any particular part of the country. That is entirely logical, since they do promote by direct-mail advertising and deliver the service at popular sites all over the commercial landscape.

The promotion of seminars and workshops readily lends itself to exploitation by the executive moonlighter. He or she probably has been the consumer of these services for many years, has developed a fascination with the production and profitability sides of it, and may be perfectly capable of putting one together.

In fact, there are new fortunes made every time a major new product comes to market. Money is made first by marketing the product and next by selling a host of associated services that piggyback their own particular specialty onto the momentum of the product or concept itself. When personal computers hit the popular market, they were followed by specialty publications to inform their users, carry advertising for the thousands of supporting products, and provide a communications channel for the consumers, developers, and manufacturers. Not far behind were the seminar and trade show promoters who provided similar services with the added twist of face-to-face participation.

As an executive moonlighter, you will operate from the perspective of the fox in the proverbial chicken coop—you are still primarily a consumer with your finger on the pulse of what interests your peers within a given industry or community. By providing what they want, you enter the realm of the seminar promoter; and there is an infinite number of ways to approach the situation.

DEVELOPING A SEMINAR

If your time for personal involvement is minimal, or you simply want to test a concept with little risk, you might consider acting as a broker. Do your homework to determine the need to be addressed, the number of participants you could reasonably attract—most come from within 100 miles of the seminar site—and the price you could command. Next, evaluate the facilities available to you and the kind of financial arrangements that might be made with their owner. Finally, approach one of the firms that regularly fills your in-basket with promotional literature and see what they would charge to package and provide an in-house seminar meeting your specifications.

There is obviously a multitude of variables to be considered, but the basic concept is sound and within your abilities to develop while retaining your full-time position. In simplest terms,

> **As a moonlighting seminar and trade show promoter you will:**
> - Identify an area of market interest that will attract a group of people willing to pay to learn more about some special skill, product, or service.
> - Appraise the competition and determine that you can offer something sufficiently different or better to capture a share of the market.
> - Establish that there is a sufficient quality pool of exhibitors or presenters to attract paying attendees.
> - Consider the impact of your promotions on your current primary employer and resolve any potential conflicts.
> - Contact national promotional services and determine whether they can produce your events for you more profitably and effectively than you can independently.
> - Consider syndication as a means of raising the capital needed to promote a seminar or trade show.
> - Use computerized databases and other such services to survey the market for fresh ideas and material for your events.
> - Identify emerging topics, specialties, and personalities that are not yet established in either the seminar or trade show markets and proceed to meet the need.
> - Establish contacts in the industry that are receptive to your ideas and willing to work with you on a cooperative basis.
> - Collect an appropriate fee for your services, which may range from a finder's fee, to a syndication share, to regular business profit from a self-promoted event.
> - Expand your base with further contacts and referrals.

Figure 6: Overview of Seminar and Trade Show Promotion

the spread between the cost of the seminar and the fees that you can collect are your profit. The more you are willing and able to do yourself, the greater your share of the proceeds. Your skills in marketing the seminar and negotiating vendor agreements to accept payment on the day of the event, avoiding costly advance payments, will also be factors in determining your success.

After you have tried something reasonably simple and experienced a measure of success, you may want to consider taking on an event of some more substantial proportions. If that is your goal, you will require operating funds and money for such things as deposits to insure the delivery of essential services when you need them.

One way to accomplish this is by using the concept of syndication described in Chapter 5 of this book. After you have gained enough experience to command the respect of a few prosperous individual investors, you should be able to draft a presentation that will show a nice profit for you and your investors within a rather short time span, as compared with most other investments. It will be necessary to respect the laws of your state and the federal securities regulators who limit pooled financial ventures for a lot of good reasons, but with that done there is every reason for you to succeed in packaging a successful venture using your after-hours effort and expertise and other people's money.

DEVELOPING A TRADE SHOW

The similarity between making arrangements and selling booths at a trade show event and putting together a seminar is clear. In either situation you identify a small, specialized market segment that is not being served effectively by the mass-market promoters. When you have done that, you must decide next whether you are better off settling for essentially a finder's or broker's fee and turning the effort over to the pros, or going forward with the major effort and all that it entails—including dramatic differences in profit-and-loss potential.

If you would be interested in attending a seminar on how to put on a trade show, contact the National Association of Exposition Managers Inc., 334 East Garfield Road, P. O. Box 377, Aurora, OH 44202-0377 (216-562-8255), and they will provide you with details. They will also put you in touch with someone in your city or region who is involved in such undertakings.

Here is a sample list of the inexpensive, practical publications they have available:

- Care and Feeding of Speakers
- Checklist for Hall Contracts
- Display Rules and Regulations
- Foreign Expositions
- Hotel/Client Agreement Guidelines and Information
- Insurance
- Introduction to Trade Show Marketing
- Legal Matters
- Marketing/Sales
- Negotiations/Contracts
- Promotion/Printing
- Registration/Computers
- Security/Safety
- Service Contractors/Services/Labor
- Shipping
- The Book of Survey Techniques

... and many, many more insider topics that will be invaluable as you examine the potential of this moonlighting field.

Another national association that might provide you with helpful contacts and information is the International Exhibitors Association, 5103-B Backlick Road, Annandale, Virginia 22003 (703-941-3725). Among their services is sponsorship of an annual trade show *about* trade shows. These associations and others with more specific constituencies are listed in the *Encyclopedia of Associations* at your local library. Contacting them can lead to referrals that will provide you with the detailed answers you seek.

Still another way to test the market for a seminar idea that may occur to you is the nonprofit route. Practically every part of the country has a college or university with a department of continuing education or some other organizational entity that is in the business of providing short-term, popular learning experiences.

Many of these institutions have become very entrepreneurial in their approach to offering such services, and you may very well structure a deal that can translate into a profit for you and exposure for them. They have the facilities for parking and accommodating a group of people. Many of them can also provide for meals and lodging in their own facilities; this is especially true of major state universities that are often equipped with complete conference facilities and staffs to handle every aspect of the promotion.

Association with a venerable institution is a good way to add stature and respectability to your venture. Local community colleges are also worth looking into. What they may lack in convention centers and ivy covered walls may be more than compensated for by prime locations and the ability to accommodate you with a minimum of complications. An excellent source of low-cost publications that relate to seminar planning, marketing, and operation in the nonprofit arena is an organization called LERN, Learning Resources Network, 1554 Hayes Drive, Manhatten, KS 66502. Their catalog is available upon request.

If you are at a loss to find an authoritative speaker, look no further than your local bookstore or library. For openers, all publishing houses have publicists who would be pleased to put you in contact with the author, or his or her agent, if there is a book that would seem to provide the basis for a seminar you would like to promote. There are also speakers' bureaus in major cities that are adept at making such arrangements. Never forget to verify the platform competency of the person you have in mind; being a best-selling author is not necessarily any guarantee that the person can spend the better part of a day before an audience without putting them to sleep.

The scope of the seminar and training industry becomes apparent when you review the volume of promotional literature that they put in the mail every year. One of the industry leaders claims to have more than a million satisfied customers from over 100,000 companies. Another provides training to over 350,000 people a year in 400 cities from coast to coast. A third flyer attests to the fact that their trainers have presented more than 7000 seminars to more than 600,000 people in the past decade. Self-promoted individuals claim to have reached nearly 200,000 people with their lectures, seminars, and workshops.

None of these figures begins to reflect the impact of the prestige establishment institutions in the seminar industry, which include such well known entities as the American Management Association and The Conference Board. Add to them the thousands of colleges and universities that are also in the business, and you get some feel for the scope of the market and the breadth of people's interest.

As a moonlighting executive with an interest in experiencing the offering side of this industry, you enjoy the advantage of being able to sit back and survey it with the wisdom gained from being an insider and a consumer. You have no need to fear the competition, because you are not really out to take them on head-to-head. In anything as large as the adult education market, there is room for a perceptive player to identify an underexploited aspect of the field and meet the need efficiently as an executive moonlighter.

Chapter 10

Computer-Related Services

There are two types of people in the world today: those who have used computers and those who have not. It may sound trite, but that fact represents a real dichotomy in the way we live our lives and run our businesses. Granted, there are light years between my very applied personal computer skills and those of the consultant we hire to install and keep humming and upgraded a small network of them at the office. But even with that limited familiarity, I have a saleable talent among those who have yet to touch a keyboard or crack a user's manual.

My pharmacist entered the computer age early on and proudly runs his business around it every day. My attorney sends me very cost-effective and unpretentious-looking bills generated on a small office system designed to keep track of billable hours efficiently. He couldn't live without it.

My dentist is still in the blurry Ozalid age, sending barely legible, tissue-thin purple bills produced on the system he inherited when he bought his practice 20 years ago. He is a prime candidate for a moonlighting computer consultant who could bring him into the modern era for a few thousand dollars.

Even a local Christmas tree farm owner I know was sensitive to the desirability of computerizing everything from her mailing lists to her crop inventory a few years ago. When I returned the next season a system was in place—selected and installed by a moonlighting executive.

The business is out there, and it exists at every possible level of sophistication. You can break it down into two basic approaches: There are those who perform services for others on the provider's own computer, and there are others who advise their clients on the selection and use of computers for the performance of their own work. Both options offer a rich array of possibilities for the moonlighting, computer-literate executive capable of producing looks of wonder merely by knowing how to plug the components together and flip on the switches. It really gets impressive when you pop in the disks and demonstrate how completely and simply the menus and manuals are written.

Depending on your own full-time place in the world-of-work, conflict of interest should be easy to avoid in this line of moonlighting. Unless you are already working for a computer development company and choose to pursue similar effort, there is plenty of room to diversify.

OFF-THE-SHELF OPPORTUNITIES

With computer software being as powerful and specialized as it is, you could begin your search for a specialty by combing through the available off-the-shelf products. If you are inclined toward mathematical projections and the representation of business financial scenarios, consider one of the advanced spreadsheet software packages that will work on your home or office computer. With a little bit of effort you can uncover what are known as *templates* that make it easy for you to approach specialized problems using basic software rather than writing a program yourself.

As a moonlighting computer-related services provider, you will:

- Select an aspect of computer-related services that can be marketed for a fee.
- Appraise the competition and determine that you can offer something sufficiently different or better to capture a share of the market.
- Establish that there is a sufficient potential demand for the services you intend to offer.
- Consider the impact of your moonlighting endeavor on your current primary employer and resolve any potential conflicts.
- Make your particular services known to the users by advertising or direct contact with potential clients.
- Use your knowledge of popular computer hardware and software to make recommendations to clients and assist them in learning to install and operate the systems, if this is your area of interest.
- Market your skill as one who knows how to navigate vast electronic databases for research purposes, if that is your inclination.
- Establish reciprocal contacts in complementary segments of the market that will steer potential clients to you for your unique applications of computer-related services.
- Collect an appropriate fee for your services on a consulting or production basis.
- Expand your base with further contacts and referrals.

Figure 7: An Overview of Computer-Related Services

Just one example of such a specialized application of business financial projections is in the area of real estate investment. If you don't already know how to handle the software in this environment, take the time to learn. After you become conversant in jargon of the field and know how to plug it in to the formulas, it is just a matter of doing so and being able to display and explain the results.

Marketing such a service might be as simple as getting yourself scheduled as the next speaker at one of the local real estate investment clubs in your area. Give your talk, provide some handouts demonstrating what it can do for the kinds of situations you know your audience is dealing with, and include a list of your fees. Stay after the meeting to conduct several actual demonstrations, and you will almost certainly walk away with some business.

Lots of people in many fields of endeavor will welcome a good, clean, relatively inexpensive solution to a specialized problem. It needs to be simply presented both in terms of their input and the useful product that they will walk away with. The mystery of the computer and its software is the magic that occurs between understanding the problem and providing the solution. You are the expert who will generate that solution without their having to worry about it or go to the expense of purchasing and maintaining the computer equipment for what amounts to an occasional use.

The services you can perform in the real estate field are but one example of how you can take an identifiable area of popular interest and tap it by offering specialized services. The task is no more complex than researching the popular computer literature, selecting software, making a list of what you can do, getting proficient at doing it, and then taking it to the potential buyers. Do that at their meeting places, in their publications, and by direct mail. Soon, word-of-mouth will carry the day and business will be seeking you out.

The parallels for doing the same kind of thing in a field other than real estate should be obvious. Pick a specialty that you are either proficient in already or in which you have sufficient interest to learn. Check for an identifiable group of users who would be likely to consider buying your service. Proceed to the computer software reviews and find some applications that do a nice job of solving the problems you know these people face.

If you have not done so already, go to a good library and start looking through the back issues of the popular computer magazines. You will find critical reviews of software designed to do literally anything from compose music to fly a private plane into

JFK Airport using instruments—and everything in between. You will easily learn what hardware is needed to support what you are trying to do and what it costs. Conversations with a few good salespeople in the computer stores will give you the pros and cons of the various systems, and you are on your way. If you are a complete novice, buy a little consulting time from someone who knows personal computers well already.

The question always arises, "If it is so darned easy, why aren't my potential clients already doing it for themselves?" The answer is always the same. The ones who *are* will not be your clients; but many, many people are so busy doing their thing profitably that they don't have the time or the inclination to figure out how to provide all of their own services. The personal computer revolution has provided you with a unique opportunity to offer powerful expert services as a moonlighting executive. You already have the general knowledge of how the business world operates and how to present yourself and your service. The specialized knowledge and equipment can be purchased off-the-shelf very inexpensively. You learn to operate it expertly, present it effectively, and profit accordingly.

What seems obvious to you as a computer-literate manager or professional can still bring wonder to the eyes of much of the population. If you like computers and what they will do, there is a world of opportunity waiting for you. Affordable technology allows you to walk in with a portable unit and produce results on the spot—or gather the data by telephone, modem, or fax from across the country, create your clients' products, and return them the same way. I cannot stress too much the tremendous possibilities in this limitless field.

ARTISTIC APPLICATIONS

If your interests run more to the artistic, rather than the business and quantitative, consider desktop publishing. A whole new industry has sprung to life in the past few years because personal computers using the right software, a laser printer, and maybe a scanner to transform art and photographs to the computer screen, can literally let you produce sophisticated newsletters, books, or anything else from a desktop.

There still are many people out there who produce printed products the old-fashioned way, although that is changing rapidly. There will always be businesses and individuals who need to have their ideas and information presented clearly at a reasonable price. With a personal computer and some desktop publishing software, you can meet their needs profitably. The degree of complexity can vary as widely as you like; Black and white or color? Line drawings or scanned photographs? Elaborate lettering or standard typefaces? Clip art or custom illustrations? These are but a few of the choices available in the realm of popular personal computer software, hardware, and peripheral equipment.

Using the artistic capabilities of computing, you literally can become a computer artist, if you are so inclined—and talented. The technology exists in the popular arena for you to create drawings and paintings on the computer. They are now the subject of shows at prestigious galleries. Composers of music can have their scores transformed directly from the instrument to written musical notation simply by *playing* the music on an instrument connected to the computer.

Again, all of this is available at popular prices. It opens avenues of moonlighting endeavor that transcend the heretofore humdrum world of the second job. You have the capacity to stretch your imagination in an almost limitless manner, become an expert in an esoteric—perhaps artistic—specialty, and ply your new trade either as the artist or an expert consultant to the artists. The knowledge is on the shelf—get yourself to the library and page through the popular computing literature until you find an application that excites you, and put it to work!

COMPUTER RESEARCH

Another field that contrasts rather sharply with the creative applications just discussed is computer research for a fee. If you have, or are willing to obtain, the basic computer skills and equipment necessary to access them, vast electronic libraries are waiting to be tapped. I have listed points of contact for several of the better known national information services in Chapter 14. Just three of many are *GEnie, The Source,* and *CompuServe,* all registered trademarks of electronic information services that you reach by modem—a blackbox that lets your personal computer talk to the database or another computer via the telephone lines.

The user fees and ranges of available information vary widely among the service companies. You can get about as specialized as necessary to meet your intended requirements. It is possible to get real-time news from the wire services. It can operate as an electronic clipping service and actually collect references for your areas of interest as they occur. Standard reference guides, such as those used to research newspapers, books, and magazines in libraries, can be available to you electronically.

When I began my research for this book, I used such a database to identify books and articles of possible interest. Part of it was done with the assistance of a moonlighting librarian who was well worth her modest fee. Some of it I did personally using the computerized research facilities of the Library of Congress and a local university library. I briefly attempted to search the old fashioned way using the thick, out-of-date published guides in the library. I did not take long to develop an appreciation for the value and efficiency of the electronic databases.

This kind of research can take many forms. I know of a firm that researches case law and statutes for attorneys. Another has created its own elaborate electronic file, consisting of thousands of sources of college financial aid, which it markets to students as an alternative to using outdated books in which they have difficulty isolating the few sources that might be interested in their particular backgrounds and aspirations. Physicians and other busy professionals have information requirements that can often be met by the skillful manipulation of electronic databases. The same is true of small and mid-sized companies that want to know things about products and services they are considering providing.

There are few fields of endeavor available to the executive moonlighter that are better suited to the professional temperament and lifestyle than computer-related services. If the general concept interests you, but you lack specific skills or equipment, do not despair. Another side of the personal computer revolution that is somewhat unique is the phenomenal job that the industry does in making its products usable, if you will only try. There are myriad small businesses—many of them moonlighting executives—teaching classes on how to use certain kinds of computers and software. Stop by your local computer store and inquire. Many times these classes are available free or at a reduced price when you purchase equipment or software.

Aside from the industry, the users themselves organize to help each other. Your computer dealer can put you in touch with a local users' group. Or you can join national users' organizations with their own publications and software libraries. A call to the headquarters of any major equipment or software manufacturer will also link you with organizations that are built around the efficient use of their particular products. Help is everywhere, and there is no excuse for not proceeding to identify a specialty and become proficient in it, if you are so inclined.

CONSULTING

Yet another approach to making money as an executive moonlighter in the broader personal computer industry is as a consultant. There is always a market for the skills of someone who knows more about computers than the user. That extends the market from my dentist, mentioned at the beginning of this chapter, who would probably consider me an expert for being able to suggest a simple system to keep his records and do his billing, to the small businessman who needs his off-the-shelf software modified to really meet his needs—a programming task well beyond my capabilities.

As a professional person with the hands-on knowledge of how data are used in the modern business world, you are in a unique position to identify and capitalize on some reasonably specialized and sophisticated moonlighting opportunities. You are a product of the information age; and, if not already expert, you are poised uniquely to acquire the specialized skills necessary to define needs and meet them. No new knowledge has to be created. Your role is to bridge the gap between the creator and the user. As an executive moonlighter, you possess the ability to communicate and command respect at both ends of the spectrum, learning the necessary specialized skills to make your role a useful one for all concerned.

Your fee arrangements will vary with the services you provide. Specific products many be priced individually. Consulting time is priced by the hour or the day—possibly by the project. Research is typically charged on a time basis, your own time and the connect time used in researching the electronic databases.

Keep in mind that the ideas related here are only the tip of the iceberg. Use them as a general construct in which you can fashion your own unique array of services that take advantage of your skills, knowledge, and interests. Ideas for the executive moonlighter are no further away than your nearest computer magazine.

Chapter 11

Success Stories

The truest measure of a concept such as executive moonlighting is to be found in the lives of the people who put it into practice. My research and observations over several years have made me aware of dozens of successful executive moonlighters. They are women and men who, while holding down—and usually excelling in—a conventional management-level or professional position, have also experienced significant success in a second career that they operate in the after hours of their working lives.

LUXURY MOONLIGHTERS

An airline pilot based in the mid-Atlantic region of the United States turned out to be a very energetic and successful executive recruiter during his non-flying hours. Granted, he has a more flexible schedule than your eight-to-five sort of professional moonlighter, but he had other things to work around, such as long trips and layovers that would have made it impossible to operate a less flexible business.

As it is, he concentrates most of his volume calling on those days when he is at home between trips. When on the road, other than the hours actually in the cockpit flying the airplane, he is perfectly capable of checking his answering service and returning calls just like any other businessperson who frequents airport lounges. While he had no desire or intention to give up flying, this pilot had established another interest in his life that provided a new professional dimension, an excellent source of additional income that he chose to use for investment purposes, and a sense of security in knowing that he had another marketable skill, should he ever find himself unable to pursue his physically demanding primary calling.

While on the subject of airline pilots, two more come to mind who represent interesting studies in the practice of high-level moonlighting. One is a Florida-based international airline pilot with a schedule that takes him regularly to the far reaches of South America. He chose to pursue a physically active moonlighting investment that combined land speculation and farming in his after hours. As the owner/operator of a commercial-grade lime orchard in South Florida, this man found an outlet for his energies, a profitable farm business, and a way to position himself in what he and his partner interpreted to be the path of future development.

In the opposite corner of the country, I encountered a third commercial pilot while we were both awaiting our flights at the Jacksonville, Florida airport. His story is not significantly different from those of the other two pilots, but the context in which it was told says a lot about the importance of moonlighting among these kinds of workers.

They have what most of us unquestionably consider to be a glamorous profession. The money is good and there is seldom any apparent reason for discontent. Why then do they go in for moonlighting ventures? Personal satisfaction and validation of worth in another area of life seem to be the primary reasons, although profit remains an important way of keeping score.

The morning in Jacksonville began with a small group of

crew members and me awaiting the arrival of a connecting flight. Big news that morning was the unprecedented failure the day before of an Aloha Airlines 737 that looked like an open convertible as it made a miracle landing on Maui. By any reasonable estimate of human behavior, that would be expected to be the dominant topic of conversation in the coming hour. It started out that way, but that topic was quickly dropped in favor of a far more lively and enduring discussion—the pilot's sugar maple farm in New England.

Engineering knowledge of the Boeing 737 paled in terms of interest when it came to his description of the age of the giant maples and his role in the centuries-old process of tapping their wealth and preparing it for market. He opened his large briefcase, and between the charts and technical data for the flight back home was nestled a row of sugar maple syrup cans emblazoned with his logo and the name of his farm—a source of no less pride than the pilot wings on his jacket.

NECESSITY MOONLIGHTERS

Okay, so much for highly paid guys with very flexible schedules who need an outlet for their entrepreneurial energies and egos. Contrast them with my next example, an association executive in Washington, D.C. who juggles a schedule of regular business travel that includes international destinations on occasion, and a full day at the office every nontravel business day. To make things worse, he carries financial burdens that include paying off debts from a failed business venture and the continuing demands of a farm he and his wife brought back from the weeds and cannot bear to part with despite its location beyond practical commuting distance from his present work.

Take the limitations just noted, add the fact that this man's profession is in the not-for-profit side of the economy, and you have the perfect setting for some near compulsory executive moonlighting. Significant financial investment or a high-profile effort of any kind were both out of the question. Further, it would simply be unacceptable for him to exploit his full-time skills in a routine consulting capacity, even though there was some demand for his services. The answer was found by calling on skills learned in his brief but intense experience as a franchise owner in the executive recruiting field.

While he did not care for the work, he knew the profit potential and had the training and initial contacts necessary to activate the business. His past experience had demonstrated that it was a very proactive pursuit that depended far more on his initiative in making calls than it did on having an office or even a receptionist to accommodate incoming calls or visitors. He was able to leave the office and arrive home each day in time to place an hour's worth of calls in his own eastern time zone and, personal energy permitting, some more in the western calling regions.

After a few months of persistence, leads developed, as they almost surely must in this frustrating, but essentially simple, business. Within the year he had placed one person and collected a fee of around $10,000—enough to pay the bills and buy additional time to line up more business.

Never happy with the constant calling, this moonlighting executive was working because of necessity, not some higher order need. He chose a commercial specialty far removed from his own professional world, learned the jargon, and, with more than his share of frustrating reversals, was able to bill over $20,000 the following year. When I last checked, a single placement had yielded close to $30,000. The deal had been closed from a hotel telephone while traveling on behalf of his primary employer. With the dollars flowing, this moonlighter was closer to his eventual goal of positioning himself financially to pursue still other interests.

This example of the after-hours effort directed toward a special and limited purpose is not at all uncommon. Age and stage of life also are major determinants in the motivation of executive moonlighters.

TRANSITIONING MOONLIGHTERS

One husband-and-wife team I encountered were both holding down full-time managerial and professional positions and planning their mutual escape to an independent lifestyle as soon as possible. They had a home and young children and had experienced several false starts at achieving their goals in full-time ventures. While their moonlighting approach was dictated by necessity, it provided the contacts and financial base needed to make what has now become a successful transition into photography and computer-related businesses in which they are prospering.

The wife had been working as a manager in a local specialty product manufacturing plant. As her children grew more independent, she found it possible to begin putting together a consulting service that sold her newly acquired knowledge of personal computing to local business and professional people. In time, she developed enough business to employ computer studies students from the local community college on a part-time basis. Soon they were routinely going to the offices of doctors and dentists to set up turnkey operations based on simple personal computers and off-the-shelf software that worked relative miracles for the appointment, billing, and other office management tasks.

As her moonlighting business prospered, she was the first to leave her professional position and bring the business to the fully operational level. In the meantime, her husband maintained his position with a state college that provided the wide range of employee benefits and security that were still important to their growing family. He also continued to moonlight by assisting his wife, trying his hand at developing real estate, and finally settling successfully on commercial photography—a lifelong avocation that was finally fashioned into a source of stable income sufficient to permit their complete metamorphosis from executive moonlighters into independent business people.

It all depends on your goals. Their ultimate objectives differed significantly from both those of the pilots and the association executive who meet their objectives short of leaving their full-time positions.

Yet another stage of life and another moonlighting objective is represented by an East Coast manufacturing executive who was an engineer with a very specialized sort of equipment expertise. As retirement neared, he found himself nicely positioned in life, but short of the personal satisfaction that he had hoped to feel at this point.

He was a well paid professional with a comfortable lifestyle, but too near the end of the career path to welcome another involuntary relocation. He and his wife had already been asked to relocate temporarily to another region of the country and had done so for nearly a year. It was not a bad experience, but they did not want to do it again. As it turned out, his greatest value in the marketplace seemed now to be his knowledge of how to install specialized equipment.

The answer for this senior engineer was a brief stint as a moonlighting consultant that paved the way for a comfortable early retirement with all of the consulting and world travel that he cared to pursue. The difference from his full-time career was the ability to work from the comfort of his own home and travel to places that he and his wife wanted to go. By the skillful application of executive moonlighting, he was able to avoid the unwanted pressures of being farmed out to troubleshoot when and where his company chose. Instead he put in place a reduced overall working schedule of his choosing. In so doing, he preserved an active lifestyle, but he did it *his* way, with the added dignity and prestige of being in demand and operating in a freelance mode.

Consulting offers an endless variety of executive moonlighting possibilities. I see it operating on both ends of the age continuum in the field of editorial services, for example.

One man who came to my attention once held major positions in the specialized publications field—newsletters, limited market newspapers, and such things. He gradually made the transition from full-time employment to something approaching semi-retirement. His current schedule is a totally flexible one, but he is in demand and spends most of his days doing what he always did. Now, however, it is on his own terms and often involves working from the comfort of his own home. For him it has been a way to avoid retirement and stay active in what he has always loved to do, not to mention the continuing income that makes it possible to accompany his still actively employed spouse on business trips to Europe and Asia.

The younger editorial consultants are a husband-and-wife team. She was a retail manager, and he had an entry-level management position with a large service firm in Washington. In spite of a total lack of any technical background, they developed a real facility with the word-processing and illustration capabilities of the personal computers available at their respective offices.

The wife was approached to prepare a simple report and brochure for a local business. She was amazed at the ease of the task and the high satisfaction expressed by the customer. Evenings and weekends of moonlighting effort eventually became a full-time endeavor for the wife, who is now developing it within the context of a government program to encourage the development of businesses by women. Before this became more than a moonlighting effort for the couple, they were sufficiently successful to learn firsthand the bittersweet side of small business success—a hefty settlement with the Internal Revenue Service.

They got themselves established, survived, and prospered largely due to their moonlighting approach to it all. The primary employers exposed them to the computer equipment and skills and allowed its discreet use after hours. When the tax man came calling, they had the financial strength of their full-time jobs to sustain them while business cash flow was temporarily diverted to pay a bill that might have ruined them in a traditional small business start-up.

BIG LEAGUE MOONLIGHTERS

Public speaking is a moonlighting specialty that is now dominating the professional activity of a former high-level appointed government official whose fortunes wax and wane with the party in power. During a hiatus several years ago, he returned to the full-time consulting business, but found himself increasingly standing before audiences around the country. He was very good at explaining, in his own unique style, the likely impact of current trends on the businesses of his listeners. As demand for his presentations began to exceed the availability of time to present it, his fees reached the $2000-a-day level; and his calendar remained full. With a hundred days a year billed at that level, his current career is more lucrative than the government positions he used to hold.

When you leave the obvious conflict-of-interest areas of the government and look into consulting firms and other less structured organizations, speaking honoraria and time off from the job to do it are a recognized part of professional compensation. In the case just described, the individual began his moonlighting in just such a fashion. He had a reputation for flamboyance and a definite knack for taking otherwise dry reports of statistics and trends and bringing them to life. Not only did he give them life, he took the trouble—never a difficult task—to make them fit the concerns of the particular audience. Each presentation took on a tone and emphasis that was unique, even though the overhead projections were the same.

Never relying on any fancy presentation materials or equipment, this speaker did his thing with colored pens on clear acetate and used an overhead projector to put it before the audience. It was his unique gift to take the current data reported by government and private-sector trend watchers and translate them into timely advice for audiences who paid to hear him give substance to what they already envisioned and hoped. He gave legitimacy to their professional causes. He told them what they wanted to hear, but in a sophisticated way. He found a need and met it, both professionally and as a moonlighter whose earnings eventually far outstripped those of his full-time consulting endeavors.

In a completely different setting from the political city of Washington where wheeling and dealing is as expected as the changing of the seasons and the leadership, I found several big-league examples of the moonlighting executive. This was long before I ever thought about the term or experienced it in my own life. As a young college administrator, my daily commute to the campus took me through the back roads and beautiful rolling farms of the central Shenandoah Valley of Virginia. One of my fascinations, as my wife and I struggled to find a way to make a down payment on a dilapidated fixer-upper farm, was with the stories I heard of who owned the various properties that I admired and how they had prospered enough to own them. Three of the stories come back to me now as excellent illustrations of what was to emerge and gain increasing attention as executive moonlighting.

One was of a young attorney who recognized the senseless inefficiency of the way legal research was being done, so he set about to computerize the process. While he pursued his livelihood on a full-time basis, he began the process that was to culminate in a legal consulting and research firm with an international clientele. Although he would probably cringe at the analogy, what I saw him do was to reduce volumes of case law to a key word search process similar to a library's *Reader's Guide to Periodic Literature,* or other references and electronic databases that let you access vast stores of knowledge with relative ease. He started it all in the executive moonlighting mode and saw it grow into an industry.

In my second story, after-hours thinking about doing business in an idyllic setting led to a nationally promoted tax-shelter plan that made its originator a wealthy man. While still working full time, this person became an increasingly active syndicator of horse farms and breeding stock. What began as a relatively simple investment-packaging scheme, which catered to area physicians and other people of means, grew into a sophisticated presentation involving national advertising, elaborate ongoing research to stay ahead of the tax laws, and vast property holdings. When the tax shelter business finally fell out of favor in recent years, his fortune had been made and another moonlighting executive had made his mark outside the organization.

A final story from my list is that of a local industrial manager who saw the need for regional trade shows for dealers to make their latest products known to retailers and consumers. While still retaining his main position, the man and his wife developed a very successful, ongoing seasonal business that eventually made them prosperous and independent—and gave *this* aspiring moonlighter something to dream about as he began his own period of testing the after-hours opportunities within his grasp.

In another example from another side of the consulting business and from the heartland of America, *Business Week* (Byrne, 1987) relates the story of a full-time manager with several *Fortune* 500 companies who took a decade to build a prosperous practice. By maintaining the firm foundation of his regular career, this man was able to build an industrial training consulting practice that eventually booked 200 days of business a year at $850 each for a very respectable annual gross of $170,000. Not a bad income by anyone's standards, and one that was unabashedly built as an executive moonlighter moving up the regular career ladder with a series of major firms.

Many more examples abound, and they are certainly not limited to the fields I have chosen to highlight as appropriate to the moonlighting executive during the present era. As I drew on my experience to give you a cross section of examples of women and men who have taken this approach successfully, I was impressed with how readily available they were in the realm of everyday professional living. It was not at all necessary to approach the rich and famous to illustrate my point.

JOIN THE RANKS

With your awareness now somewhat heightened by reading this book and this chapter on the specific examples, I would be willing to bet that situations in your own experience are coming to mind. You will not have to look far to uncover executive moonlighters in your midst. They are a respectable and productive group of your peers who have gotten the entrepreneurial itch so common in our times. But rather than opting for a radical departure from their comfortable, upper-middle-class lifestyles, they choose to spend their energies, at least initially, in the after hours of otherwise busy and successful lives.

Executive moonlighting remains sort of an underground economy of the clean variety. Most of its practitioners are well scrubbed and nicely turned out members of our society's professional and managerial class. They operate their after-hours enterprises legally, pay their taxes, and generally seek to avoid anything that would disrupt their otherwise well ordered lives. It is an interesting commentary on our times and institutions that so many people so nicely situated would choose to spend their energies trying to craft an enterprise of their own for such a multitude of generally higher order reasons. As the currently popular comedian explains in his Eastern Bloc refugee dialect: "What a country!!!"

What a country, indeed. And what a time in which to live. The prosperity, the well ordered society, the freedom, the burgeoning service economy, and the consumer access to incredibly sophisticated and yet affordable technology lets you step into the big leagues with relative ease and comfort. If you have an idea and the will to try it, few legitimate excuses exist to prevent you from taking the next step and pursuing your dream. Never before has it been possible to do so on such a significant level with such minimal investment and risk.

Do not let the fact that there is no job application to complete stop you from pursuing your goal. That veil of ambiguity is often the final obstacle separating the doers from the dreamers. Most of the other traditional obstacles have fallen by the wayside. Financial risk has all but been removed for the executive moonlighter, as has the necessity to disrupt your career and way of living. All that is left as a firm requirement is the determination to proceed with the one-step-after-the-other process that is implementation.

Research your concept and take the necessary precautions

discussed throughout this book to keep from putting yourself seriously at risk—then go for it! What have you got to lose? Worst case is the less-than-horrendous discovery that you really *do* prefer the paycheck and sick days and the ability to leave it all behind when the day is done. Best case finds you in command of a whole new world of independence, prosperity, and personal fulfillment. Something in between the two is a perfectly worthy goal.

Chapter 12

Business Basics

Every year thousands of people yield to their entrepreneurial desires and launch business ventures of their own. For some, it is a dream come true—for others, something less. It becomes a life-changing total disaster for the least fortunate and a road filled with unanticipated new directions for many others who get back on track only after an uneasy period of recovery and reflection.

Going into business is *serious* business, and you need a down-to-earth grasp of some of the basics before you take the plunge. Too often, people dreaming of starting their own company get locked into a mode of thinking that is mainly castles in the air. That is to say, they are all too eager to hear what they want to hear. Things like motivational literature take on a validity that is only partially warranted. Rational critics are perceived as naysayers and are brushed aside in favor of listening with too much rapture to the people who stand to profit from their investing in certain products and services.

With the moonlighting approach, you will still need to incorporate certain traditional business considerations, but with quite a different twist from that of your full-time counterparts.

This chapter is intended to introduce you to basic business requirements while helping you avoid the unnecessary complexity that may doom your venture.

HOW NOT TO START A BUSINESS

I entered the executive recruiting business some years ago as a full-time, heavily indebted franchise owner/operator. It was a great way to learn the business and get a fast start, but for me it was more than I needed or could afford. Within six months I found myself painfully undercapitalized and trying to survive in the middle of the deepest recession since the Great Depression. Before sinking all the way, I scrambled and found an interim full-time position that stopped the financial hemorrhaging; and, within a matter of months, I was recruiting *my* way—part time with a full-time salary to keep the noteholders happy and my sleep peaceful.

I was back in my world again, and it made all the difference in my ability to succeed at the business. With financial stability and my old self-image restored, I was able to approach my after-hours recruiting with a degree of professionalism and effectiveness that quickly surpassed anything I had done on a strained full-time basis. I was now relaxed and confident. I needed to succeed, but it was no longer life-and-death. I defined a narrow specialty and successfully covered whole regions of the country within it.

Best of all, I did it successfully. Operating an hour or so a day, several days a week, caused some lengthy intervals between fees, but periodic $10,000 checks from satisfied clients sustained my recovery. I had started in executive recruiting with the misperception that I needed to be part of a national organization and have a prime business address, elaborate telephone equipment, and traditional office hours. I quickly learned that it was all unnecessary as I became an executive moonlighter, an approach I urge you to emulate as you begin your exploration of earning serious money outside of the corporate workplace.

KEEP IT SIMPLE

Off-the-shelf word processing software and some of the least costly personal computers and printers on the market today will produce thoroughly professional correspondence, resumes, cover letters, fee letters, invoices, and most of what you will need for whatever business you plan to operate. After you grow, you may find it useful to have a database package to manage your files and a spreadsheet or accounting program to help with the bookkeeping, but all of that can come later. In the beginning, and until you are truly overwhelmed by the growth of your business, stick to the basics and do not waste time or resources on fancy equipment and procedures.

The three things that are absolutely essential are: (1) A good telephone with a "call-waiting" feature, so you'll know if someone is trying to reach you while you are on the phone (no need to pay for two lines!); (2) a quality answering machine that will let the caller comfortably leave a long message, if necessary, and that you can page from other phones around the city or the country, if you travel; and (3) a word processor that will let you produce professional quality reports and correspondence. That is it! Do not waste money on more than that. There are a million tempting things to try, and they are not going to help enough to matter. Consider them rewards for when you are comfortably established and can afford the luxury. Examples of tempting, nice-to-haves include:

- Specialized software and computer systems that cater to your particular industry. Forget it until you are so absolutely overrun with business that you cannot live without custom support. The marketplace is full of outstanding, easy-to-use personal computers and software that can meet your needs very inexpensively for a long time to come, whether you are an executive recruiter, a desktop publisher, or some sophisticated financial consultant.

- Telephone gadgetry such as speaker phones, headsets, automatic dialers, bug detectors, etc. Most modern telephones sold at the local discount store will dial an access code to a long distance service, if you even need that. Speaker phones usually sound like you are talking from the bottom of a well—hardly a professional image for a person whose image is his or her telephone impression. A headset is tempting, especially if it has an amplifier, but given the choice between these things and staying financially comfortable and totally committed to the business at hand—making those business calls and plenty of them—I say when in doubt, do without!

TASK AVOIDANCE

To this day I suffer from what one of my trainers in the executive recruiting franchise called "analysis paralysis." If I am not extremely careful and disciplined, I will sit down at the telephone for an afternoon of calling and think myself into the ground. There are endless ways to complicate something, and I am gifted at running every last one of them through my mind—with the very best of intentions! All I am doing is preparing thoroughly for the task at hand. Right? Emphatically, W R O N G! This can be a problem for the analytical, critical thinking manager or professional. If that describes you, learn to overcome it.

Whether you are functioning as an executive moonlighter in recruiting or almost any other field, one of your main challenges will be to focus really meaningful effort on the money-making aspects of your business during the limited time that you can devote to it. *Reasonable* preparation is needed and acceptable. You should think about what you are doing and approach the task with a degree of order and insight. Excessive thinking will grind you to a painful and unprofitable halt! You will have to be very candid with yourself about what you are really doing, if you find yourself avoiding making the necessary calls or performing the other business tasks that you find less than enjoyable.

Think of it this way. Reasonable preparation assumed, you are going to get a lot more accomplished in a dozen imperfect calls than in half as many intricately thought-out calls. In the final analysis, your success will depend on uncovering new situations and interests that will lead to actual business, be it recruitment and placement or securing a lucrative consulting assignment.

You must always remind yourself that the calls are not related, from the perspective of the person being called. There is no logical basis for building up dread or negative feelings about calling. The people you call almost certainly have no idea that you just made a similar call, or a few dozen of them, and either did or did not meet with success. They neither know nor care. It is a new situation each time, and you must remember that and keep on calling. The person who really wants to hear what you have to say may be waiting at the next call. You are practicing a very simple craft—aided by your ever increasing knowledge of your specialty and the people who work in it—but always dependent on communicating with them constantly.

If this sounds too much like selling and you find that objectionable, you had better consider seriously the fact that few new enterprises make it without being marketed energetically. Whether promoting your services as a computer researcher or a money broker, don't count on the phone ringing *in* to you very often until you have made it ring *out* to potential clients a lot more times. Starting a new business is a very proactive task. You are your business, and your energy is all that will give it life. That holds true for full-time and moonlighting enterprises alike.

I know of people who were number one at role playing in their franchise training class, had beautiful offices waiting for them back home, and still failed miserably because they could not face the task of getting on the telephone every day and generating business. In time, if you build an organization, you will be motivating others to do that task for you; but as a start up it will unquestionably fall to you. As an executive moonlighter operating solo, you are the one who has to pick up that phone and find the business.

It amazes me how few business and professional people recognize that this personal marketing is such a crucial role for the entrepreneur. I guess they are functioning in protected specialized roles deep within established organizations and just don't appreciate the fact that it all had to start somewhere with someone asking for the clients' business. Executive moonlighting is a fine way to discover whether you can (and are willing to) perform this essential function until your business gets established and generates enough demand for your services not to *need* marketing. Keep in mind that in most businesses that point is never reached.

It is this sometimes difficult aspect of energizing a business that really makes it all possible for the executive moonlighter. More than anything else, this phenomenon is what lets you reach out to any corner of the land and grab business away from the complacent folks in full-time jobs who just do not ask as thoroughly or as persistently or as convincingly or as well as you do. They may not reach down into the marketplace as far as you will, or they may just not do it often enough to ask for the business at the moment the service is needed. Do that enough times, and you will make money.

Many calls will result in a brusque "no thank you" or "I cannot help you with what you are looking for today" response. Most people are usually quite polite, if you don't wear out your welcome. The treasure lies in catching that relatively small percentage of your specialized contacts who, at the moment you reach them, are in need your services. The only way to determine that is to contact them on a regular basis. The most efficient way to do so is by initiating a quick, businesslike telephone call. Nothing complex. Nothing to dread, avoid, or think to death—just call the people!

There is always a mailing you can prepare, files you can reorder, or shopping you can do. Plenty of people will talk with you about nonbusiness matters. There are walks you can take—or naps, for that matter. All of this is fine because you are your own boss. Just understand the impact that doing anything other than your primary business activity—making calls to potential clients—will have on your probability of making a profit selling your service. While you are *thinking* about it, someone else may be *doing* it. While you are preparing the perfect approach, someone else may blunder in and snare the project you longed for. All of the extras are privileged activity for those who can afford it. They are paid for with the profits of the business, and there had better be some profit if you intend to succeed.

When all is said and done, you will make it or not on your ability to focus your necessarily limited time and energies on those few activities that really matter. If you have planned your moonlighting venture adequately, what you need to do to make money is clear. Direct your attention to those limited specific tasks, and you will surely make the fees I have described. The intervals between fees are more affected by the number of calls that you make than any other single factor, given reasonable preparation and skills. Profitably providing a business service is really very simple. Never overlook or complicate that reality and you will do quite well.

ORGANIZATION, REGULATION, AND TAXATION

Even though it may just be you, a telephone, and a personal computer working out of your own study, it will be necessary to adopt a form of business organization, comply with all applicable regulations, and not overlook any legal taxation. With that said, let me urge you to keep all of this in perspective.

You will have a certain grace period wherein you can try some things without a lot of concern for business formalities. Be ready to fall in line the minute you make money or start claiming business expenses that can affect your tax picture. Minor problems can occur when the small start up has failed to file the necessary paperwork with state and local regulators. For example, you do not want to do high profile things that will bring local attention to your efforts such as having clients or delivery people come to your home office in numbers sufficient to alter the character of your residential neighborhood—especially the parking.

Your best bet is to do the honorable thing as soon as you feel that you are going to be doing sustained business in your moonlighting specialty: Go down to city hall and sign up as a consultant. Keep it very simple and avoid trying to be some special kind of something that will require you to satisfy a lot more requirements, post bonds, take tests, or who knows what else. If you plan to do executive recruiting, it is very easy to get lumped in with the employment agency people and a whole set of regulations that have nothing to do with the business as you will practice it—never charging a fee of those you place, for example.

If you are going into any form of brokering or syndication, take the trouble to read the local codes and figure out what you may be forbidden to do without certain licenses. In most cases, you can define a role for yourself that will steer clear of the requirements that were never intended for people like you anyway, but it is important to know the laws and comply. Seek an attorney's advice if you are at all uncertain, but explain to him or her that you are really doing a simple, limited thing on the side and what you seek is advice to help you avoid trouble.

Taxation is a fairly simple matter for the executive moonlighter who will probably just file a "Schedule C" with his or her regular federal income-tax return to report any income or loss from his or her business activities. While it probably never was a really good idea to lose money for income tax avoidance purposes, it has become a very bad one since the recent changes in the tax laws. That is not to say that you should not claim legitimate business expenses and even take the loss if it is clearly part of a potentially profitable venture, but be prudent. Consult a respectable accountant about the limits for car, travel, entertainment, in-home office, and other expenses that are red flags to tax auditors. If you meet the tests, take the expenses; but you will be well advised to spend your energies trying to make money to pay taxes on rather than plotting how to avoid those levies.

Plan to get the opinion of an attorney and a tax accountant

early in your business venture. Never avoid doing so after you start making money. There are more ways to bring on penalties and audits than you want to know. No one is telling you to love the tax office, but it is counterproductive to fight it. Make your plans early in your business career to comply with the laws, because there simply is no other way. The audits are very much for real and they can ruin you. Ignorance is no excuse. When you undertake to become an independent businessperson, you are obligated to know. I suffered an audit that cost me about $15,000 and lasted nearly three years when I could least afford the time or the money; and it involved no penalties—just an honest error in accounting judgment.

Your decision on your form of business organization will be an outgrowth of taxation and liability laws. I will not attempt to advise you on legal or accounting matters that are better left to professionals in those fields. My only counsel is to keep things simple and honest. When your business grows to the point where a more complex form of organization is warranted, it is a simple matter to adopt a proper form of incorporation or whatever is appropriate.

Libraries and bookstores are full of good books on small business organization. The Small Business Administration provides many publications at no charge. All you need to do in the beginning is make sure that you have taken care of the minimal registration and taxation requirements and are not operating in conflict with any laws or regulations. With that done, forget about the fine points; and concentrate on making your business work. When your business begins to make money, devote some of the early profits to buying some good legal and accounting advice on how to proceed with your growing enterprise.

Chapter 13
Ethical Considerations

The attitudes of management toward the practice of moonlighting vary widely and are certainly in transition. You will want to make an accurate appraisal of the impact of your after-hours endeavors on your prospects at your place of full-time work before you decide just what approach will be the best one for you.

The decision you face is rarely one of whether you will be able to become an executive moonlighter. It is more apt to center on the question of how closely your after-hours work should relate to your primary job. As demonstrated in earlier chapters, there are many choices for putting distance between the two. A second consideration that will depend to a large extent on the attitudes at work is how open you will be about your moonlighting. If necessary, a very low profile can be adopted. Only you can judge what is desirable in your circumstances.

Before discussing the policies that guide some companies and the sorts of conflicts that you might possibly face, let's look at what really should guide your practices as an executive moonlighter. There are certain common-sense lines that should not be crossed, regardless of the policies in your firm:

- Trading on the proprietary information of your employer is wrong, and you should never base your business on doing that.

- Using substantial company time or resources to accomplish personal business objectives is unacceptable.

- Doing anything that serves to weaken the competitive position of your employer is not an acceptable basis for your moonlighting business.

These are obviously broad, general points that are subject to a lot of interpretation. You are the person who must exercise that judgment when it comes to practicing your executive moonlighting in the same commercial world as your primary employer. When in doubt, opt for a greater distance between your venture and any implication of conflict with the main job. There is plenty of room to range freely without treading on areas that may lead to bad feelings or worse. The same good judgment must be exercised when it comes to the use of your personal energy. Simply put, save enough for an unrestricted effort at the office and plan to slip in your moonlighting obligations, or deal with them remotely, when duty calls.

There are companies that will admire your initiative and even try to incorporate your efforts into those of their business if you are sufficiently successful. The *Wall Street Journal* (Hymowitz, 1983) described a moonlighting computer sales professional who started a sideline of helping his customers select and customize their equipment. He did so well that his sales increased and at last report he was considering merging his business with that of his employer.

Other firms state clearly that moonlighting is prohibited and will not be tolerated among their professional employees, although more are accepting the practice if it does not detract from expected performance. Few employers are actually able to prevent you from doing something that is not an obvious conflict of interest on your own time, but you will have to respect the impact that it may have on how you are viewed by those who control your career.

Computer Decisions (Lasden, 1983) published an extensive survey of moonlighting practices and policies in that industry. It reported that about 10 percent of the computer firms outrightly prohibit moonlighting and that it is viewed as unacceptable in many more. It was a subject of considerable controversy, and double standards existed with managers doing extracurricular consulting while finding the same behavior unacceptable in their workers. Nearly one in three managers surveyed admitted to moonlighting.

If you will respect and self-enforce the common-sense rules called for in working for yourself and another firm simultaneously, there is an excellent chance that executive moonlighting will actually make you a better company person. Instead of internalizing a lot of subtle resentment and becoming an unhappy, trapped member of the team, you may instead view the job as the fine, if limited, opportunity that it is and happily give it your best.

In-house politics will matter less, and you will be better insulated from the kinds of limitations that stem from playing them without appropriate detachment. You will have the growing confidence that you can succeed without the organization if necessary. Just knowing *that* often results in the kind of refreshing confidence that is appreciated in the organization and actually opens doors closed to the more uptight members of the group. Others have found that moonlighting exposes them to current practices in their specialty that they can actually apply to the main employer to their mutual benefit.

It probably is never a good idea to make your executive moonlighting activities a high-profile thing that can bring on resentment or unwarranted scrutiny. If it becomes the subject of an inquiry, be honest and especially humble about your sideline. This is not the time to seek the ego gratification that may be a longer range goal. Explain it as little more than a hobby, certainly nothing that would threaten or detract from your future with the firm. Few would impair your right to try such a thing if it doesn't hinder your performance or pose a conflict of interest.

Most people will not take your efforts seriously even if they become aware of them. There is a "Junior Achievement" perspective that you may find your efforts interpreted as during the start-up phase. Welcome it. The more it is viewed as an Amway-type venture, the less threatening it will be to those with whom you continue to interact. Accept their downgrading with good humor. When and if your venture becomes something significant, that will be more than apparent and you will then be in a position both to command respect for your venture and decide which direction to take if a choice is forced. You don't want to upset any carts or burn any bridges until that point is reached.

It would rarely be acceptable to use any excess time at the office to actually do more than think about a personal venture in that setting, but there is surely no rule that says you have to spend your personal time thinking only company thoughts. The same is true for those who travel. There are long hours in airports and planes and evenings in the hotel that, after you have done an honest job for the primary employer, can effectively be devoted to planning an endeavor of your choosing. There is no widely accepted presumption that it is less respectable to make calls or prepare written materials relating to a moonlighting venture during these hours than it is to sleep, read, pursue a sport—or hang out at the bar.

For those inclined to appreciate such things, there are few pleasures more gratifying than savoring the thrill of closing a deal of your own from the other coast after an honest day of doing business for your primary employer. The charge of adrenaline that pulses through you for Job One also provides the energy you need for success in Job Two. It becomes a win/win situation.

While I don't advocate advertising the fact that you are moonlighting in such a way as to mix roles, there is nothing fundamentally wrong with doing it if you are an honest operator who doesn't give in to the temptation of such false economies as charging personal business calls to the employer's credit card, and so on. Such practices are a false economy and are totally unnecessary. Run your business honestly. Establish the necessary credit to operate it professionally, independently, and honestly. Keep the tax records straight; and be prepared to face an audit forthrightly when your unconventional earning and expense patterns bring you to the IRS computer's attention, as they inevitably may.

There is a confidence that will accrue to the genuine benefit of your employer and you as you grow into a person of dual capabilities performing in two distinct areas with the sense that the world wouldn't end tomorrow if either of them went away. On the day you awake with the priceless assurance that you can make it either way, you'll almost certainly be better at both jobs for having that knowledge born of true personal accomplishment.

While few will aspire to the Pulitzer Prize as a goal of their moonlighting ventures, perhaps you can gain useful perspective on the potential for solid, ethical, and socially valued behavior in the realm of the after-hours executive, if you remember the thinking of one man who achieved that lofty end. The late poet Wallace Stevens responded to a colleague's questioning about the ethics of jotting down an occasional line or two of poetry on company time by saying that his Sunday afternoon walks in the park often contained thoughts about actuarial tables; and he felt, therefore, that it all tended to come out about even! (Blackburn, 1988) In the final analysis, there is no effective mind control; and *we* must be the arbiters of who justly pays for and profits from our thoughts.

Chapter 14

Sources of Additional Information

This section is intended as a sampling of the many materials that are available to help you establish and expand your executive moonlighting business. Within the list itself are sources that will provide you with expanded lists on various specialized areas. Many of the firms have telephone numbers, so you can verify quickly whether or not their products and services would be of interest to you. If you plan to write, it is best to use your business letterhead or include a business card to show that you are a bona fide potential buyer.

All of these sources are believed to be current, and the organizations named are legitimate to the best of my knowledge; but you should exercise the same kind of consumer awareness that you would with any purchase. Satisfy yourself that the firm provides what you seek at prices and under conditions that you find fair. By listing them here, I neither endorse nor stand behind their products and services, although I know from personal experience that many of them are excellent.

ASSOCIATIONS

This is a listing of some of the more prominent professional associations that relate to many of the specialties discussed. You may want to consider joining them, examining their ethical guidelines, or otherwise consulting them for information on the fields they represent. Consider this list to be only a sampling, and consult the *Encyclopedia of Associations* under your areas of interest for an exhaustive, annotated listing.

Association of Executive Search Consultants, 151 Railroad Ave, Greenwich, CT 06840 203-661-6606

Employment Management Association, Box 2598, Raleigh, NC 27602 919-828-6614

Institute of Management Consultants, 19 W. 44th Street, New York, NY 10036

National Association of Executive Recruiters, 5881 Leesburg Pike #303, Falls Church, VA 22041 703-998-8450

National Association of Exposition Managers, 334 E. Garfield Road, Aurora, OH 44202-0377 216-562-8255

National Association of Personnel Consultants, 1432 Duke Street, Alexandria, VA 22314 703-684-0180

National Speakers Association, 4747 N. Seventh Street, Suite 310, Phoenix, AZ 85014 602-265-1001

BOOKS AND MANUALS

Following are some publications that may prove useful to you in establishing your business. There are many more like them, and I suggest examining the offerings of some of the free book catalogs mentioned. Don't overlook the newsletter and other sections of this chapter. Some of the books mentioned may be found in libraries, especially the major reference works. Many of the listings are limited-circulation, how-to-do-it publications that you will have to buy, if you decide a copy would be useful. It may be worth a trip to the reference section of a major library or a visit to a business that might use the specialized publication that you are considering before actually making the purchase. Some publishers will provide the names of subscribers in your city where you might examine a copy of their books. Most items can be ordered through the publishers, and their addresses are available at your library. No attempt has been made to list the readily available standard business references.

Beguelin, Richard H. *The Secrets of Syndication.* Little, Brown and Company, Boston, 1985, 287pp. $18.95. A thorough overview of syndication as a way of doing business and a complete how-to-do-it on the subject. The last 100 pages is a set of specific proposals presented as syndicated packages. Must reading for anyone considering syndication.

Closing on Objections, Research Information Bureau, PO Box 9653, Kirkwood, MO 63122. Tips on how to close a deal in the recruiting business. $20.00

Consultants Bookstore Catalog, ERN, Templeton Road, Fitzwilliam, NH 03447 603-585-2200. Free catalog of suggested readings in management consulting and executive recruiting. Very useful. All the books listed are available from this source.

Corporate Finance Bluebook, 163 West 74th Street, New York, NY 10023 212-496-0555. Detailed listings of contacts-by-name in 17 areas of finance at top 4500 corporations.

Dunne's National Directories of Professional & Executive Recruiters, PO Box 6255 FDR Station, New York, NY 10150 212-570-2992. Inexpensive directories of recruiters by areas of specialization. They will list you at no cost.

E/M Resource Directory, Employment Marketplace, PO Box 31112, St. Louis, MO 63131. Over 1000 suppliers, vendors, and providers of goods and services to the placement industry. $40.00

Entrepreneur, 2392 Morse Avenue, P. O. Box 19787, Irvine, CA

92714-6234. 800-421-2300 (800-352-7449 CA residents). Detailed start-up manuals for a variety of full-time businesses, many of which would not fall in the moonlighting executive's probable areas of interest. However, the manuals are excellent and economical sources of amazingly detailed insider information and basic business good sense. I highly recommend calling their toll-free number and letting them tell you what they have available in your specialty—there are 250 or more from which to choose. At the very least, it is a treasure trove of ideas to consider. Expect to sift through a lot of chaff to find a few grains of interest, but it is a worthwhile exercise. Here are some examples of manuals that you would find worth considering if you are interested in any of the fields discussed in earlier chapters of this book:

Executive Recruiting Service, Manual No. X1228, $59.50

Financial Broker, Manual No. X1962, $75.00

Information Broker, Manual No. 1237, $64.50

Consulting Business, Manual No. 1151, $59.50

There is also a selection of computer-related services ranging from desktop publishing to retailing. They sell a series of manuals on improving your business skills and knowledge that are valuable if you need that kind of assistance. It is a very nuts-and-bolts approach.

Grilli, T. Robert, *How to Become a Money Broker*, Diversified Financing, PO Box 283, Lincoln, RI 02865. 401-353-2180 (office), 401-353-4171 (residence). Mr. Grilli will sell you a publication that gives you the benefit of his lengthy experience in the field, including lending sources, for $49.

Koek, Karin E. and Martin, Susan Boyles, Eds. *Encyclopedia of Associations*, 22nd ed., Detroit: Gale Research Company,

1988. This is the place to find the association that has been formed to represent whatever business specialty that you have selected. It lists over 6000 such organizations. A good library will have it.

Marlow, Cecilia Ann and Thomas, Robert C., Eds. *The Directory of Directories,* 4th ed., Detroit: Gale Research Company, 1987. When you want to find clients for any business, this is the place to start. It will guide you to publications that contain detailed listings of practitioners in various businesses and specialties. It is a multivolume set showing information on approximately 9600 such publications. Available at your library.

McFadden Business Publications, 6195 Crooked Creek Road, Norcross, GA 30092-3196 404-448-1011. Publishes Directory of American Financial Institutions, American Bank Directory, etc. Approximately $135 (call for current prices).

Nursing Job Guide/Nursing Job News, Prime National Publishing Corporation, 470 Boston Post Road, Weston, MA 02193 617-899-2702. Thousands of hospital hiring officials nationwide.

Personnel Publications, PO Box 301, Huntington, NY 11743 516-427-3680. How-to-interview books giving the right questions to ask for over 70 job categories and a basic understanding of the job functions of the people you will work with in these fields.

Placement Strategy Handbook, Allen & Hawkinson, Search Research Institute, PO Box 49931, Los Angeles, CA 90049 "...167 pages of practical and useful advice ... candid, honest solutions to the real-world problems of working a desk." $32.50

The Recruiting & Search Report, Kenneth J. Cole, Publisher, PO Box 9433, Panama City Beach, FL 32407 904-235-3733. Primarily a newsletter for executive recruiters, the organization is also a rich source of consulting and information research books and publications. Ask for their list of available publications.

Ward's Business Directory, 11 Davis Drive, Belmont, CA 94002; Ed Martin 800-227-8431 for information. Industry listings for 90,000 firms.

Who's Who in Recruiter Computers? The Kimberly Organization, PO Box 31112, St. Louis, MO 63131 314-965-0291. Compilation of 85 companies whose products are designed with the recruiting and placement professional in mind. $15.00

ELECTRONIC DATABASES

Whether you are planning a moonlighting venture as an information service provider or simply want to do research for another business or personal requirement, here are the names and addresses of three of the leading firms operating electronic databases.

CompuServe, 5000 Arlington Centre Blvd., PO Box 20212, Columbus, OH 43220 614-457-0802 or 800-848-8199. An H & R Block company that has been supplying extensive information services to *Fortune* 500 companies since 1969—available to you on a subscription-fee basis.

GEnie, GE Consumer Services, Department 02B, 401 North Washington Street, Rockville, MD 20850 800-638-9636. The General Electric Network for Information Exchange (GEnie) provides a variety of services via your telephone modem and computer.

The Source, 1616 Anderson Road, McLean, VA 22102 703-734-7500 or 800-336-3366. An extensive selection of communication and information services for access via your computer and telephone.

FRANCHISES

While franchises are generally offered as full-time business propositions, they do represent a wealth of operational information on what the marketplace is currently supporting. If it would be helpful for you to know more about a given business specialty, visit a franchise fair or buy a popular listing at your newsstand. Send for some information and talk to some franchise firms if you need to know more about what is involved in the business that interests you and what costs can be anticipated. Depending on your circumstances, it may be possible for you to engage in a franchise opportunity as an executive moonlighter owner with a working manager. Following are several examples in the executive recruiting area; comparable listings can be found in most business specialties.

Bryant Bureau, 4000 S. Tamiami Trail, Sarasota, FL 33581

Dunhill Personnel System, One Old Country Road, Carle Place, NY 11514

Management Recruiters, 1127 Euclid Ave., #1400, Cleveland OH 44115-1638

MATERIALS & MISCELLANEOUS SERVICES

This is a catch-all category that you will have to examine item-by-item. It is full of things that you may find useful as you establish yourself and grow in a moonlighting business. Some will have no relevance to your situation, so I urge you to keep it simple and select only what you may need. Save the others as things to consider when your growing practice requires them. My intent is to give you some idea of the scope of specialized services available to you.

Allen, Jeffrey G., J.D., C.P.C., Second Floor, 10401 Venice Blvd, Los Angeles, CA 90034 800-445-3272/213-836-2500/714-

851-2100. A national law practice specializing in the recruiting and placement industry.

American Business Lists, Inc., PO Box 27347, Omaha, NE 68127 402-331-7169. Business lists by any *Yellow Pages* title from over 4800 telephone directories nationally. Useful if you are trying to identify clients for your services in other cities.

Arch S. Whitehead Associates, Inc. 845 West End Avenue, Suite 15C, New York, NY 10025 212-316-1400. Detailed directories and individual searches for marketing/sales personnel in any industry—thorough, but expensive.

Business Travel News Travel Manager Salary & Career Survey, John Conkling, Research Dept., CMP Publications, Inc., 600 Community Drive, Manhasset, NY 11030. $45. Survey of 400 business travel managers (not a list of their names) by publishers of a trade newspaper for the business travel industry. Illustrative of the kinds of specialized publications that will let you access an industry.

Communications Channels, Inc., 6255 Barfield Road Atlanta, GA 30328 404-256-9800. CCI publishes about 50 industrial, business, real estate, and consumer periodicals and directories. Ask for a list of their publications. Topics include adhesives, airline executives, building design, art materials, containers, fence industry, health foods, paint & coatings, real estate, rubber, shopping center world, robotics, pension, trust & estates, waste equipment, and so on. Some include directories of companies and their officers. Useful in identifying people with whom you might do business.

Plan Management, Inc., 9420 Annapolis Road, Suite 205, Lanham, MD 20706 301-459-3044. Errors & omissions insurance for the placement industry.

RSE Marketing, Route 1, Box 435, Weyers Cave, VA 24486. You will receive a sample executive recruiting job order, candidate interview form, fee letter, invoice, candidate preparation handout, fact sheet, and scripts for both recruiting and marketing. $10.00.

Shana's Endeavors, PO Box 693, Cupertino, CA 95015 408-866-5250. Research service for hi-tech companies in the San Francisco Bay Area—detailed lists of contacts at 1000 companies, 5000 names, updated regularly.

World Wide Facilities, Inc., 300 Garden City Plaza, Garden City, NY 11530. 800-645-6068 (516-248-5000 in NY). Errors & omissions insurance for the placement industry.

NETWORKS

If you find that you do not like working alone, here are some of the companies that will help you link up with others doing the same kind of recruiting around the country. They can certainly expand your reach, if you find an organization in which you can be comfortable. It is a less restrictive and costly alternative to at least one of the services provided by many of the franchises.

Career Network, Computer Search International Corporation, 1500 Sulgrave Ave., Baltimore, MD 21209 301-664-1000. An electronic mail-based listing of jobs and candidates.

First International Personnel Consultants, Inc., PO Box 720114, Atlanta, GA 30358 404-256-2025. Computerized candidate data bank.

Insurance National Search, Personnel Associates, 731 James Street, Syracuse, NY 13203 315-422-0070. An electronic mail interchange for insurance industry recruiters.

Inter-City Personnel Associates, PO Box 2275, Appleton, WI 54913 414-739-7788. A network of independently owned agencies that share job orders and resumes.

National Personnel Associates, 150 Fountain Street, NE, Grand Rapids, MI 49503 616-459-5861. An independent recruiting network that shares job orders and resumes nationally.

NJM National Network, PO Box 286, Kensington, MD 20895 301-946-8910. Resume exchange and job market newspaper.

NEWSLETTERS & PERIODIC PUBLICATIONS

These are the ongoing sources of current information in the executive recruiting business. They will illustrate what is available in this industry. Similar publications can be found for almost any specialty by consulting a newsletter directory at the library. If you are interested in knowing how others operate and what is available to you in a world of constantly changing services and products, these are your sources.

Employment Marketplace, PO Box 31112, St. Louis, MO 63131. A free, quarterly listing of products and services for the recruiting, search, and employment professional.

Executive Recruiter News, Templeton Road, Fitzwilliam, NH 03447 603-585-2200. Newsletter for executive recruiting, management consulting, and outplacement industries. Sample issue $2; $77 per year. Directories and bookstore catalog.

Fordyce Letter, PO Box 31011, St Louis, MO 63131 314-965-3883. Monthly newsletter for recruiting and placement industry. About $75 per year.

Micro Moonlighter, 2115 Bernard Avenue, Nashville, TN. A monthly newsletter for people who do after hours work with their personal computers.

National Business Employment Weekly, 420 Lexington Ave., New York, NY 10170 212-808-6796. *Wall Street Journal* weekly job listings.

National Job Market, 10406 Muir Place, Kensington, MD 20895 301-946-8910. Weekly job summary newspaper.

Nationwide Careers, 800-458-5859. Weekly guide to professional advancement opportunities.

Recruiting & Search Report, PO Box 9433, Panama City Beach, FL 32407 904-235-3733. Interesting, free newsletter and an outstanding source of practical publications (sold via mail order) for the search and recruitment industry, but of interest to anyone who needs to make contacts nationally. Examples of what they have available: "The Basic Research Shelf"—a set of 3 publications that includes a *National Directory of Addresses & Telephone Numbers, Who Runs the Corporate 1,000* and *Knowing Where to Look—Ultimate Guide to Research*; also a guide to *Independent Researchers & Services* (a directory of people who will assist you in finding information for a fee); books on recruiter methods and techniques, compensation, retainer search agreements, and so on. Write for details.

EXECUTIVE RECRUITER TRAINING

In Chapter 4, I provided you with an overview of the executive recruiting business as it can be practiced as a moonlighter. If you want further training in detailed operation of the business, here are some companies that specialize in providing such services.

Bruno System For Success, Placement Marketing Group, PO Box 41008, St. Louis, MO 63141. 250 pages of information new consultants require, tabbed format, looseleaf binder, scripts, checklists, etc. $195; 11 audio tapes are an additional $195 (both for $340).

Peter Leffkowitz, Morgan Consulting Group, Inc., 6800 College Blvd., Suite 550, Overland Park, KS 66211 913-491-3434. Script manual for use during calls. Tabs lead to scripts for any situation. $349, videotape an additional $79.

Pritchard Marketing Group, PO Box 209, Bala Cynwyd, PA 19004. *Fundamentals of Recruiting* audio tapes. $79.95

Professional Search Seminars, Steven M. Finkel, President, 11901 Olive, Suite 212, St. Louis, MO 63141 314-991-3177. Highly regarded trainer in the industry. Professionally produced videotape programs on techniques and management of a placement business; in-house training and consultation available. A worthwhile seminar for about $50—call and see when it is scheduled near you.

The Pros, 50 Briar Hollow Lane, Suite 290 W, Houston, TX 77027 713-621-3161. Tapes and videos for the recruiting profession.

Ratio:1, Ginger Thaxton, 32 Sea Breeze Lane, Bristol, RI 02809 401-846-3880. Training tapes for recruitment and management.

Bibliography

Atchison, Sandra D. "These Top Executives Work Where They Play." *Business Week*, No. 2970, 132-134 (October 27, 1986).

Bamford, Janet. "Managers in Chains." *Forbes*, **138** (25), 134-136 (August 25, 1986).

Blackburn, Charles. "Juggling Careers: When One Job Isn't Enough." *Pace*, **XV** (VIII), 38-40 (August, 1988).

Bohlen, Celestine. "Soviets Take on Moonlighting." *The Washington Post*, p. A21, (June 22, 1986).

Byrne, John A. "Before You Hang Out A Consultant's Shingle." *Business Week*, No. 3027, 138-139 (November 23, 1987).

Byrne, John A. "Business Is Bountiful for Elite Headhunters." *Business Week*, No. 3047, 28 (April 18, 1988).

Current Population Survey, Bureau of Labor Statistics, U. S. Department of Labor, Washington, May, 1985.

"Dual Careers," *Wall Street Journal*, p. 33, (June 2, 1987).

Fraser, Bruce W. "The Moonlight Shines on White Collars." *Nation's Business,* **71**(7), 52-53 (July, 1983).

Fromm, Erich. *Escape From Freedom,* New York: Avon Library, 1965.

Holland, John L. *The Self-Directed Search Professional Manual - 1985 Edition.* Odessa, FL: Psychological Assessment Resources, Inc., 1985, 96 pages.

Hymowitz, Carol. "Wearing Two Hats: More Managers Try Moonlighting to Boost Income and Fulfillment." *Wall Street Journal,* p.1 (August 9, 1983).

Jamal, Muhammad. "Is Moonlighting Mired In Myths?" *Personnel Journal,* **67**(5), 48-53 (May, 1988).

Kelley, Robert E. *Consulting: The Complete Guide to a Profitable Career.* New York: Scribners, 1981.

Kiechel, III, Walter. "Passed Over." *Fortune,* **114**(8), 189-192 (October 13, 1986).

Koek, Karin E. and Martin, Susan Boyles, Eds. *Encyclopedia of Associations,* 22nd ed., Detroit: Gale Research Company, 1988.

Lasden, Martin. "Moonlighting: A Double Standard?" *Computer Decisions,* **15**(3), 83-92 (March, 1983).

Machan, Dyan. "My Partner, My Spouse." *Forbes,* **140**(13), 240-242 (December 14, 1987).

Marlow, Cecilia Ann and Thomas, Robert C., Eds. *The Directory of Directories,* 4th ed., Detroit: Gale Research Company, 1987.

Maslow, A. H. *Toward a Psychology of Being,* 2nd ed., Princeton, NJ: Van Nostrand, 1962.

McDermott, Mike, Editor. *The Franchise Handbook,* Fall 1988, Milwaukee: Enterprise Magazines, Inc., 1988.

"Moonlighting Is All The Rage." *Wall Street Journal,* p. 22, (January 11, 1985).

Mullally, John J. "Moonlighting? Even Managers Do It." *Industry Week,* **189**(12), 22-29 (June 21, 1976).

Standard Periodical Directory, 11th ed., Oxbridge Communications, Inc., 1988.

Stinson, Jr., John F. "Moonlighting by Women Jumped to Record Highs." *Monthly Labor Review,* **109**(11), 22-25 (November, 1986).

Super, Donald E. *The Psychology of Careers,* New York: Harper & Brothers, 1957, 362 pp.

Trost, Cathy. "All Work and No Play? New Study Shows How Americans View Jobs." *Wall Street Journal,* p. 19, (December 30, 1986).

Index

Accomplishment, feelings of, 14–15
Advertising, by consultants, 109
Airline pilots, moonlighters, 145–147
Ambition, unfulfilled, 14–16
American Association of State Colleges and Universities (AASCU), 109–110
American Bank Directory, 100
American Entrepreneur's Association, consulting manual, 115
Answering machines, 4, 11–12, 74, 159
Answering services, 11
Art, computerized, 140
Associations, 85, 173–174
Audition tapes of public speakers, 122
Awkward situations, executive recruiting, 62–64, 67–68

Banks:
  industry publications, 38
  loan officers, 98
  local, 97
Bed and breakfast inn syndicates, 80
Beginning of enterprise:
  consulting business, 108–109
  executive recruiting, 49–50
BLS, *see* Bureau of Labor Statistics
Bookkeeping, expert consultants, 108
Books, *see* Publications
Boredom with work, 15–16
Borrowers, 91–92
Brokering, legal restrictions, 164
Bureau of Labor Statistics (BLS), 26, 27, 30
Business declines, 17
Business practices, 1
  of special field, 36

189

Business principles, 157–165
Business-to-Business Yellow Pages, 36
Business Week, 43, 154
  on consultants, 106
  on consulting fees, 115

Capital needs, 20–22
Careers:
  boredom with, 14–16
  change of, 8–9, 31
    moonlighting as preparation, 7–9, 17
  declining business, 17
  security from 23
CareerTrack Seminars, Incorporated, 124–125
Certified Speaking Professional (CSP), 121
Challenges, 33–35
Chamber of Commerce, membership directories, 101
Characteristics, *see* Personal attributes
Choice of enterprise, 33–38
Clients, potential, 35
Closes, in executive recruiting, 60, 64–65
Colleges, training seminars held at, 132
Commerce Business Daily, 112–114
Commercial Lending Newsletter, 96
Commitment to enterprise, 41–42
Communications, in executive recruiting, 72
Communications technology, 11–12
  and money brokering, 103
Community colleges, training seminars held at, 132
Company time, use of, 168
Compensation, nonmonetary for public speakers, 122

Competition in field, 40
Computer Decisions, 169
Computer-related services, 135–143, 149, 176
  legal research, 153
Computers, 3, 27, 41
  databases, 13, 141–142, 178
  desktop publishing, 139–140
Consultant, identification as, 37, 102
Consultant Referral Service (CRS), AASCU, 109–110
Consulting, 105–116
  computer-related, 142–143, 149
  industrial training programs, 154
  as transitional business, 150–151
Consulting: The Complete Guide to a Profitable Career, Kelley, 115
Consulting firms, 112
Consumer credit, 100
Contacts, in money brokering, 101–103
Contingency fees, 41
  for money brokering, 94–95, 102
Contingency search firms, 46, 61
Corporate security, loss of, 23
Correspondence, 3
  in money brokering, 99
Costs of franchises, 78
Counseling, for career choice, 34–35
Credit unions, 100
CRS (Consultant Referral Service), AASCU, 109–110
CSP (Certified Speaking Professional), 121
Current Population Survey, 1985, 30
Customer lists, 36

Daily cycle, executive recruiting, 72–75
Databases, 13, 141–142, 178
Desktop publishing, 139–140
Directories, 35–38
 for expert consultant clients, 110
 for money brokering, 95–96, 101
Directory of Directories, 37–38, 101
Dissatisfaction as motivation, 29

Economic environment, 12
Editorial consultants, 151
Education:
 in computer applications, 142
 for executive recruiting, 183–184
 for new venture, 43–44
Educational institutions, training seminars held at, 132
Electronic databases, 13, 141–142, 178
Employees, moonlighters as, 28
Employers, and moonlighting, 75, 167–171
Encyclopedia of Associations, 105, 115, 131, 174
Entrepreneurs:
 independent, 25–26
 problems of, 31
Equipment required, 41–42, 159
Escape from Freedom, Fromm, 4
Ethical considerations, 167–171
 public speakers, 123
Executive recruiting, 2, 38–41, 45–75, 145–146, 148, 158
 legal restrictions, 164
 training seminars, 183–184
Expert consultants, 105–116

Failed ventures, 28
Fast start techniques, 43–44

Fee letters, 61, 70
Fees:
 for computer services, 141, 143
 for executive recruiting, 48, 61, 70–71
 for expert consultants, 114–116
 for money brokering, 93–95, 98, 102
 for public speakers, 121–123
 for syndication services, 82
Financial aspects of moonlighting, 21–23, 147–148
Financial requirements for franchises, 78
Focus of efforts, 160
Forms, sample, executive recruiting, 64
Franchises, 77–78, 114, 158, 179
 executive recruiting, 71
 syndication, 85
Fromm, Erich, *Escape from Freedom*, 4
Frustrations, in workplace, 14–15

Goals of moonlighters, 42–43, 150

Head-hunting, *see* Executive recruiting
Hiring offices, 51–52
Holland, John, "Self Directed Search (SDS)", 34
Home office, 13
Honesty, 75, 169–171
 in executive recruiting, 50, 56, 59–60
Hours of work, 2, 28
Idea development, 13–14

Income, from consulting, 105–106

Industry Week, 29
Information requirements for syndication, 84–86
Information services, computer databases, 141
Information sources, 35–37, 173–184
   computer-related services, 138–139
   expert consultants, 115
   money brokering, 95–96
   syndicates, 85, 87–88
Institute of Management Consultants, training course, 115
Interests of employer, 168
International Exhibitors Association, 131
Interviews:
   for career information, 39–40
   executive recruiting, 57–59
Investors for syndicates, 81–82, 86–87, 88

Jamal, Muhammad, 28
Job change, *see* Careers, change of
Job descriptions:
   computer-related services, 137
   executive recruiting, 47
   expert consultation, 107
   money brokering, 93
   professional speaking, 119
   seminar and trade show promotion, 129
   syndication, 79
Job placement industry, *see* Executive recruiting

Kelley, Robert, *Consulting: The Complete Guide to a Profitable Career*, 115

Knowledge of operation field, 35–36

Learning Resources Network (LERN), 132
Legal regulations, 163–165
   of money brokering, 93–94
   of syndicates, 86
Legal research, computerized, 153
Lenders, 91–92, 96–97
   money brokering, 101
LERN (Learning Resources Network), 132
Libraries, information from, 37–38, 174–175
   computer-related services, 138–139
   for consultants, 109, 114, 115
   for money brokering, 95–96
   for syndicates, 87–88
Lifestyle:
   changes, 18–19
   maintenance of, 25–26
Limited partnerships, money brokering restrictions, 94
Location of enterprise, 19, 35, 42–43
   of money brokering, 100
Long distance telephone operations, 35
Lowman, Rodney L., 32

Management of syndicates, 80–81, 88
Manuals, 176
Marketing of service, 39, 40–41, 161–163
   computer services, 137–138
   executive recruiting, 50–57, 66
   public speakers, 124–125
Market potential, 35
   for consultants, 106–114

Marriage, and moonlighting, 20
Maslow, A.H., *Toward a Psychology of Being*, 30–31
Mass marketing communications, 12
Materials, 179–181
Mergers, and executive recruiting, 67
Modems, 141
Money, personal need for, 20–21, 147–148
Money brokering, 91–103
Moonlighting 1–5, 155–156
　and career change, 7–9
　choice of enterprise 33–38
　incidence of, 27
　motivations for, 2, 13–21, 29–33, 147–148
　personal attributes, 25–32
　success stories, 145–156
Morris, Robert, Associates, 96
Motivations for moonlighting, 2, 13–21, 29–33
　financial necessity, 147–148
Mullally, John J., 29

National Association of Exposition Managers, Inc., 130–131
National Speakers Association (NSA), 121
Needs, special, and moonlighting, 21
Negotiations, executive recruiting, 57–60
Networking, 40, 181
New products, associated services, 128
Newsletters, 182–183
Nonmonetary compensation for public speakers, 122
Nontraditional lenders, 97
NSA (National Speakers Association), 121

Objectives of moonlighting, 33
Occupational Outlook Handbook, U.S. Government, 36
Offer of job, executive recruiting, 61
Office equipment, 159
Office technology, 13
Off-the-shelf computer applications, 136–139
Organization of business, 163, 165
Organizations:
　computer users, 142
　consulting, 105
　professional, 36–37
　　directories, 95–96
Outplacement, 17
Outside activities, encouraged by employers, 28–29
Overviews:
　of computer-related services, 137
　of executive recruiting, 47
　of expert consultation, 107
　of money brokering, 93
　of professional speaking, 119
　of seminar and trade show promotion, 129
　of syndication, 79

Performance-oriented specialties, 40
Periodical publications, 182–183
Personal attributes, 25–32, 43
　of money brokers, 91–92, 95, 99
Personal computers, 3, 27, 41, 159
　associated services, 128
Personal satisfaction, 14–15
Personnel offices, 51
Peters, Tom, 122
Physical handicaps, 21

Preparation, excessive, 160–161
Private enterprise, responses to, 5
Professional advice, 85–86, 164–165
Professional speakers, 117–126
Profits:
 from seminar promotion, 129
 from syndicates, 82–84, 89
Prohibition of moonlighting, 169
Proprietary information trading, 168
Public appearances, for consultants, 110–111
Public speaking, 117–126, 152–153
Publications, 35–38, 174–178
 consulting information, 109
 periodicals, 182–183
 professional, 95–96
 See also Libraries, information from
Publishing houses, training seminar speakers, 132

Quality of service, 9–12, 41

Real estate:
 computer services, 137–138
 money brokering restrictions, 94
 syndicates, 80
Recruiting, executive search, 53–57, 67
 See also Executive recruiting
Referrals:
 consultants, 109–110
 money brokering, 102
Relocation:
 executive search, 58
 two-career couples, 20
Research, computerized, 140–142

Resources for executive recruiting, 64–68
Résumés, in executive recruiting, 52, 56–57, 66
Retained search firms, 46–47
Retirement, 18
 and consulting, 151
Robert Morris Associates, 96
Rogers, Buck, 122
Ruse calling, 50, 62

Sales techniques, executive recruiting, 65
Sample forms, executive recruiting, 64
Satisfaction in work, 14–15, 26
 higher order, 31–32
Schedules of work, variations 27
Second job, quality of work, 9–12
Security from job, 23
"Self Directed Search (SDS)", Holland, 34
Self-knowledge, 5
Seminars, 43
 promotion of, 127–133
 public speakers for, 121
Service-oriented economy, 12
Services, availability of, 179–181
Small Business Administration, 165
Speakers, 117–126
 expert consultants as, 111
 for training seminars, 132
Speakers' bureaus, 123, 132
Special interests, 33–35
 organizations, consultants and, 111
Specialization, 35–39, 46–48
 computer services, 138
 in money brokering, 100–101
Special needs, 21
Speculative financial arrangements, 46

Splitting of fees, executive recruiting, 70–71
Standard of living, and career change, 8–9
Start-up of enterprise:
  consulting business, 108–109
  executive recruiting, 49–50
Status, and work, 8
Stevens, Wallace, 31–32, 171
Stress, in executive recruiting, 48
Success in moonlighting, 3, 145–156
  in syndication, 80
Syndicators, 77–89, 130, 153–154
  legal restrictions, 164

Taxation, 151, 164–165
Tax shelters, 87, 153–154
Technical specialties, 40
Technology for moonlighting, 3–4, 11–13
Telecommuting, 42–43
Telephone communications, 3–4, 11–13
  executive recruiting, 65–66, 68–70, 73
  long distance, 35
  marketing, 161–163
  money brokering, 99, 100
Telephones, 159–160
Terminology of specialty, 36
  of money brokering, 95
Testing of market, 13–14
Time required, 2, 42
  for executive recruiting, 72–74
  for syndication, 84–85
Toastmasters International, 120
Toward a Psychology of Being, Maslow, 30–31
Trade associations, syndicate information, 85

Trade publications, 35–38
Trade show promotions, 130–133, 154
Traditional lenders, 96–97
Training, 43–44
  for consultants, 115
  for executive recruiting, 183–184
  for public speaking, 120–121
Training seminars:
  promotion of, 127–133
  public speakers for, 124–125
Transitional businesses, 149–151
Travel expenses of public speakers, 123
Trusts and Estates, 38
Two-career couples, 20

Underutilization, as motivation, 29
United States Government:
  consulting assignments, 112–113
  Occupational Outlook Handbook, 36
Unpaid consultants, 106

Videotapes of public speakers, 122, 124
Vocational rehabilitation, 21

Wall Street Journal, 26, 27, 168
Word processing software, 159
Work:
  boredom with, 14–16
  quality in second job, 9–12
  satisfaction from, 14–15
  schedule variations, 27
  security from, 23
Workshops, 43
  promotion of 127–133
  public speakers for, 121

Yellow Pages, 36